The Good Management Guide for the Voluntary Sector

NCVO Publications

The Good Management Guide for the Voluntary Sector

John Harris

NCVO Publications • London

Published by NCVO Publications
(incorporating Bedford Square Press), imprint of the
National Council for Voluntary Organisations
Regent's Wharf, 8 All Saints Street, London N1 9RL

First published 2002

© NCVO 2002

The author and publishers would like to thank
Kogan Page Ltd for permission to reproduce
material on pages 140–1 and the developers,
copyright and trademark holders of the quality
schemes described in Chapter 4, including Charities
Evaluation Services, Investors in People UK,
Birmingham Voluntary Services Council, Tony
Farley and the British Quality Foundation.

Special thanks are due to those who as individuals
or reference groups read and made useful comments
on the work in progress.

If you have any comments on or suggestions for
this guide, please contact the author via
jmhotley@onetel.net.uk
or email ncvo@ncvo-vol.org.uk

Typeset by Q3 Bookwork, Loughborough,
Leicestershire
Printed and bound by Bookcraft, Midsomer Norton

A catalogue record for this book is available from
the British Library

ISBN 0 7199 1589 9

Contents

ABOUT THE AUTHOR

John Harris has been working in the voluntary and community sectors for 25 years. His involvement includes activism in the housing co-operative movement and community-led childcare provision. He has also been involved in mental health work (with social services) and ran Shelter's northern training programme. Since 1990 he has worked as an independent consultant and trainer to the voluntary and community sectors. This has involved working with boards of trustees, project evaluation, organisation development and direct training in management and communication skills. For the past five years he has acted as lead tutor on the course he co-developed, the "Post-graduate Certificate in Management in the Public and Voluntary Sectors" at Leeds University, the School of Continuing Education.

He also co-wrote the best-selling training manual "Managing Residential Child Care" (published by Pavilion).

Introduction

HOW THIS BOOK CAN HELP MANAGERS AND ORGANISATIONS

The workforce in the voluntary sector has been expanding faster than either the public or the private sectors. Its total paid workforce numbers 563,000.* The sector employs more women than men; more men work part-time in this sector than in either the public or the private sector; and the voluntary sector also employs more people from black and ethnic minority (BME) groups than either of the other two. The contribution made by the voluntary sector is huge – in financial terms (its total income, as reported in *The UK Voluntary Sector Almanac 2002*, is £15.6 billion); in the provision of services to people in need or suffering from social exclusion; and in terms of how the sector involves so many people from the community as unpaid workers and trustees.

Good management skills are essential in the voluntary sector, just as they are in the public and private sectors. But when, in the late 1990s, the Voluntary Sector National Training Organisation (VSNTO) researched current and predicted skills needs and shortages across Britain, one of its main findings was that 'the biggest skills gap for paid staff in the sector across England, Scotland and Wales was in the area of management'. (*Skills Matter*, VSNTO). If you are in a management position and want to see yourself, your organisation and community grow, this book will act as a creative and constructive resource. It can help you in the following ways:

- as a tool to enable you, as an individual manager, to learn and develop, to survive and thrive
- to apply your learning as a developing manager in ways that will help grow your organisation and community
- as a workbook when working towards a management qualification. Its format complements S/NVQ and other study structures

* Source – The UK Voluntary Sector Almanac 2002

- to help you find your way through a changing environment with all its pressures: funding requirements, the contract culture, the demand for innovation, quality initiatives, Best Value, partnership working, regionalisation, the Compact
- as a resource for staff or board members responsible for cultivating staff growth, by using the tried and tested development and training exercises throughout the book.

By growing staff we grow organisations; by growing organisations we grow communities.

MAKING THE MOST OF THIS BOOK

Learning objectives

Key learning objectives for each chapter are identified and explained. A number of issues affect the functioning of a person or organisation. These are explored so that you can recognise them and interpret situations in the light of this understanding, then use your learning to influence matters for the better.

Case studies

Two particular case studies are used through the book in order to illustrate ideas and approaches for dealing with different situations. Other case studies are used and linked to the relevant sections. Case studies are drawn from real life and typical situations.

Exercises

Each chapter contains exercises. These are the building blocks for your development as a manager, and for your organisation or project. Use them by yourself, with your team, with your management committee . . . but above all, use them. The exercises have been tried and tested by workers from a wide range of organisations and community groups.

A TOOL TO ENABLE YOU TO LEARN AND DEVELOP, SURVIVE AND THRIVE

A group of managers coming to the end of a course for the Certificate in Management for the Voluntary and Public Sectors posed the question: 'What will management be like in 2020?'

One of the themes that emerged in answer was the changing trends in employment. The view of the future that these managers saw was that of the 'portfolio worker' or 'knowledge worker' – someone working on short-term contracts in temporary and uncertain situations, who would have to take full responsibility for his/her own development.

This situation can be viewed in positive terms. After all, what can be wrong with the idea of skilled, knowledgeable workers toting their portfolios around and working for the highest bidder? One criticism of this model is that it is a reflection of the fragmentation of the workplace that has been occurring for some time. Is it not also appropriate, or desirable, that workers develop loyalty to organisations that set out to nurture and grow them?

We have all received the message that there are no longer any jobs for life. More than ever, managers need tools and resources to learn; put ideas into practice; and be supported in not only their survival, but in their growth and development – their potential to thrive.

As mature adults we take responsibility for our own learning and development. Lifelong Learning is a positive concept: learning new skills and acquiring knowledge is something we can do at any age or stage of life. Learning is no longer confined to school, university or college.

GROWING YOUR ORGANISATION AND COMMUNITY

Management is about doing the right things well. This book uses theory when it supports the notion that the end purpose of management is *making things work*. Managers need to make sense of their world and be able to make interventions that solve problems, help other staff, and ultimately make a difference. This book is for the manager who wants to improve performance in the workplace. Staff and organisation should be in a state of symbiosis, and the learning, developing manager should be able to contribute effectively to the growth of the organisation that pays the wages.

A WORKBOOK THAT SUPPORTS A MANAGEMENT QUALIFICATION

Links to competence models

It has long been a concern that in the United Kingdom our training and development in the workplace compares poorly with that in other European countries. However, a significant development in this respect has been the trend towards vocational qualifications. These focus on nationally recognised standards that clearly describe what the expectations are of people working in different occupations, including managers. Hence, National Vocational Qualifications (NVQs) and the Scottish equivalent (SVQs) demonstrate that people holding these are *competent* at their jobs.

A key distinction between vocational and academic qualifications is that whereas academic qualifications tend to be based on knowledge that is assessed or examined, vocational qualifications focus on performance at work, how people use their skills and knowledge and how they meet defined standards of performance. For vocational qualifications evidence has to be given to demonstrate that performance standards have been met.

Vocational qualifications for management

In 1991 vocational qualifications were introduced for management (Management Charter Initiative, *What Are Management Standards? an introduction*). The integrated structure offers seven key roles, each divided into units. Within the units are elements that describe what needs to be done in order to complete the relevant work. Each element comes with performance criteria together with the underpinning knowledge and understanding necessary for consistent performance.

Links to other study frameworks

Other study schemes aim to integrate the academic and the vocational approach. One such is the postgraduate certificate in Management in the Public and Voluntary Sectors at the University of Leeds, specifically developed for managers in the not-for-profit sectors. The programme comprises four modules: Managing Service Delivery; Personal Competencies; Managing People; and Managing Finance and Information. The scheme brings together practical and academic assessments in the context of experience of work and organisational needs.

A GUIDE TO THE CHANGING ENVIRONMENT

One crucial management skill has been defined as *environmental scanning*. Just as living organisms need to adapt to their environment to survive, so do managers, as caretakers for organisations and communities. This means being a *watcher*. A recurring theme throughout this book will be learning skills that help you watch, notice and foresee.

Both individuals and groups tend to settle into their own space, to develop their own little worlds of comfort and safety and to stop looking outside. But it is important for the voluntary sector manager to understand environmental changes in the broader context.

Funding requirements and the contract culture

The political climate changed a great deal in the 1980s and 1990s, especially with regard to the management of public services and public spending. Key themes emerged, including the separation of the roles of purchaser and provider, thereby reducing the expectation that public-sector bodies would automatically be providing services themselves. Some services had to be put out to tender through Compulsory Competitive Tendering, while others were contracted out to other agencies – very often in the voluntary sector.

Meanwhile a shift occurred from a grants-based system to one of contracts for services within a quasi market economy.

How has this affected voluntary organisations? There are concerns that users' interests come second in the contracting process – that the other side of developing clarity through contracting is increased inflexibility and larger organisations benefiting at the expense of smaller ones.

Concerns have also been raised about time-limited funding for voluntary sector projects, which makes forward planning very difficult – especially in the context of the debate about how the charity sector operates and fundraises generally. This issue is explored further in Chapter 7.

Despite such concerns, it is recognised that contracting-out also brings benefits to voluntary organisations: increased professionalisation and formalisation; clarity about the service being contracted; the development of new skills; improved lines of accountability; and a drive towards clearer goals.

Quality initiatives

These changes in culture focused on value for money whereby services should be run efficiently, effectively and economically. Thus, greater attention to quality assurance in public and voluntary services was encouraged, with a focus on standards and performance indicators as measurements of what quality looks and feels like to the customers or service users.

Best Value

With the change to a Labour government in 1997 Compulsory Competitive Tendering was replaced by Best Value. Set to be a challenging new framework to ensure that local council services continuously improve, it assesses services for funding on quality as well as price. Best Value revolves around the 'four Cs': challenge, comparison, consultation and competition (see Chapter 4).

Best Value impacts on councils and therefore on the voluntary sector. The higher the expectations placed on local authorities in this regard, the higher will be the expectations for voluntary organisations. In particular, any voluntary organisation providing a service funded by a local authority will be involved in Best Value when that service is reviewed, with reviews taking place over a five-year cycle.

Demands for innovation

A regular complaint from managers involved in the work of fundraising is the degree to which funders, whether they are trusts, foundations or local authorities, demand that the funded services be of an innovative nature. However, the work of many organisations is in addressing the needs of social exclusion, of poverty, of core distress – where the drive for innovation can feel like just one more bureaucratic imperative. In this book, this aspect of management will be considered in Chapter 5, in terms of marketing and relevant public relations initiatives.

Partnership working

The government is committed to what it calls 'joined-up thinking', and in particular the provision of 'seamless' services. This means a much closer collaboration between, for example, health services and local authorities, between the housing department and social services, between local authorities and the voluntary sector. Within the voluntary sector initiatives are being explored which involve greater partnership and collaboration between organisations, not just in service provision but also in marketing and fundraising (*NCVO Research Quarterly 2000*). Most organisations would welcome this in broad terms, but it also raises the question of resourcing – how can staff spare more and more time to attend partnership or consultative meetings when they are already over-stretched? Will extra resources be invested to build up this aspect of the sector's capacity?

The Compact

In line with the new thinking on partnerships the government has launched the Compact on Relations between Government and the Voluntary and Community Sector in England. According to the Compact booklet, 'The Compact is an expression of the commitment of Government and the voluntary and community sector to work in partnership for the betterment of society and to nurture and support voluntary and community activity.' Part of the Compact process includes publication of codes of good practice which include funding; consultation and policy appraisal; volunteering; and community groups. An annual meeting is held to review the operation of the Compact and its development.

Regionalisation

The government's regionalisation agenda is crucial to the interests of the voluntary sector. At its core has been the setting-up of Regional Chambers and Regional Development Agencies – bodies that are responsible for the creation of long-term regional strategies for economic development, physical and social regeneration and developing people's skills. Clearly there are good reasons why the voluntary sector needs to be involved in this process: the voluntary sector is a major player in terms of income generation, spending and employment and can contribute to the overall strategy for the regions. It can use the regionalisation process to develop regional structures for the voluntary sector so that there is a 'mirroring' of key voices for each region. The voluntary sector will champion excluded and minority groups as no one else will. This is a developing agenda and one to keep an eye on.

1.

Personal management competences

What is the fundamental tool of management? It is yourself. However, this is also typically the resource or tool that receives less maintenance or care than anything else.

This guide can help you reverse such neglect.

A community arts worker made the point that she found it much harder to fundraise for herself to attend a major overseas conference than to fundraise for the project she works for. Why? Because it felt selfish and could expose her to the criticism of others. Yet attending this conference would enthuse this worker and inform her work for young people for the rest of her life.

To develop this more personal aspect of managing, this chapter looks at:

- a core model for management competences
- the ability and desire to learn and understand: the thinking aspect of managing
- the art of relating and communication with others – enabling, assertion and process skills
- communication skills in groups and teams
- making the best use of your limited time and energy
- surviving when the going gets tough – stress and its management.

A CORE MODEL FOR MANAGEMENT COMPETENCES

It helps to have models to use to understand and interpret situations before we take action. If, as managers, we believe we need to develop, we also need a map to help us find our way. We may also need to recognise that in terms of development and learning there is no destination, only the journey.

What might such a map of personal management competences look like?

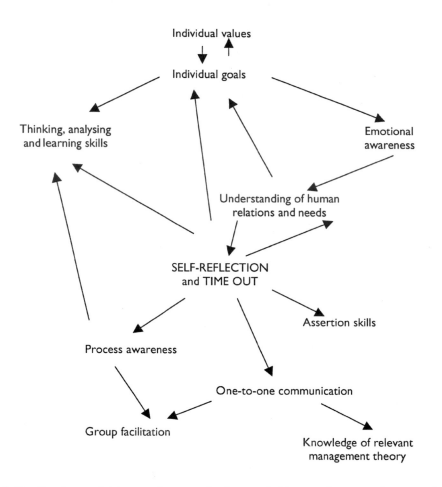

Self-reflection and 'time out' are at the heart of this complex map, because the personal competences of management rest on the realisation that there is no growth without investment in the self.

Managers seeking to meet a multitude of demands have to take the time to 'sharpen the saw' as Stephen Covey (in *Seven Habits of Highly Effective People*) describes it. Stress rears its ugly head, when individuals feel that the demands are outstripping their inner and outer resources for coping. Taking time out means spending some time, either on your own or with others, to take stock, to experience the present, to allow yourself to think and to let your plans take shape.

This has always been problematic, because for so long the cultural expectation has been that we always should look busy and appear to be in control. Taking time to assimilate rather than to do can be a challenge.

This first case study includes some food for thought about personal competences and values. It may help you to take notes as you read and think.

Case study: Housing For All (I)

HFA began as a housing provider out of a local group that had met and campaigned on homelessness issues in the 1970s. It began small, focusing on housing young, homeless people. Its first management committee was formed out of the original group and other local people. Very early in its development a local youth worker was appointed as co-ordinator. He was passionate in his commitment to young people and others in need and had very clear ideas about how to support them.

By the mid-1980s the number of staff had risen to 30, the co-ordinator had become the director, the organisation had taken on housing association status in order to access Housing Corporation funds and the housing provision had extended to supported housing for people with mental health difficulties. Over these years the director had worked tirelessly to improve and expand the service. His approach was autocratic and he would not tolerate disagreement with his decisions or style of working.

At this time public expenditure was coming under close scrutiny. The Housing Act of 1988 brought an important change in the way that development work by housing associations was funded. From being in a position of having the total costs of any scheme met by grants from the Housing Corporation, HFA now faced a situation where only a proportion of these costs were met, with the remainder having to be found by borrowing. Any overspend had to be met by the organisation's own resources.

The director met these challenges by closer supervision of staff, tightening up on procedures, reducing costs wherever possible and taking on more staff only when absolutely essential. All these measures were announced in a quarterly forum, but little explanation was given for the new developments. On being asked questions about the changes the director spoke vehemently about the 'new environment' and how the 'easy days' were over and that staff needed to 'sharpen up their act if they were to continue to justify their existence'. There was 'no room for complacency'. Team leaders were instructed to 'get tough' with individuals and to use supervision to improve performance and reduce sickness levels. If they attempted to discuss or disagree he would not listen, but simply reiterated his instructions.

From that point rumours and gossip took hold and people were continually hearing from others about a new round of cuts and redundancies to come. In one period of three months four disciplinary processes were in progress.

At this point three of the most experienced and committed staff wrote a letter to the director,

Dear Director,

We are writing to you to express our concern over the current situation. Morale has never been so low among the staff and we feel that certain things need to change if the situation is to be saved. Certainly, if significant improvements are not made then we three will have to leave.

Recently a whole range of restrictive practices have been imposed on the staff which have made working life here almost intolerable; once staff were trusted to get on with their work – now supervision is so close as to be unsupportive.

Sickness regulations have been tightened up so that people are afraid legitimately to take time off when ill, for fear of losing their credibility – or their jobs.

Costs have been cut to the bone and we are not taking on the requisite number of staff for the amount of work we have.

In HFA's recent 'forum' you announced various new measures – unfortunately in a top-down fashion which gave no opportunity for discussion.

We are extremely concerned about these developments and would like to meet with you in order to see if we can make some real improvements in this organisation. Otherwise we feel that working here will no longer be a viable option.

Yours sincerely,

The Troubled Trio

The director agreed to meet with the Troubled Trio. He had been taken aback and his first words were angry. He was furious at what regarded as the undermining of his position. He would not listen to any alternative ideas to his approach and his anger escalated. In the end, the meeting brought no resolution or relief for anyone.

Analysing the case study

It is not very difficult to identify some of the issues that arise from a consideration of the management competences and values involved in this situation. These include:

- the director is demonstrating a disastrous lack of communication skills, at both one-to-one and group levels
- a lack of skill in communicating often links to other skills and values – does the director not value the opinions of others?
- in the workplace there needs to be a balancing of rights and responsibilities – the director is denying staff some of their rights (for example, to be heard)
- the director is showing that in this situation he has little or no understanding of human relations and needs – the organisational needs have changed and need to be addressed, but will this be achieved by alienating the committed staff?
- the director is not doing too well on the level of self-reflection and time out. What he is doing is destructive, but he cannot see this. He is caught up in his own world view and interpretation and needs help in reframing – that is, seeing the situation from a new perspective and bearing in mind that a management approach that

may have been appropriate – or even vital – during the forming of the organisation, may be wholly inappropriate as it – and its staff – develop and mature.
- it is important at the level of management committee and senior management to
realise that there are also crucial issues of both structure and lack of policies and
procedures in this situation, and that the director needs support and supervision.
The management committee needs to take its responsibilities more seriously.

The following description of a model of personal management competence will help
you to avoid the pitfalls of the director.

THE ABILITY AND DESIRE TO LEARN AND UNDERSTAND: THE THINKING SIDE OF MANAGING

One of the most powerful tools of management is the ability to think constructively.
Models for learning, planning, reviewing and managing quality often have core
features in common – one of which is that the models are cyclical.

Learning

We have to be able to learn. We have to be willing to watch, to think and to understand. One view is that the only justification for the existence of managers is the
improvement of the work of their staff. The key to this is *learning and then helping
others to learn*. A very useful approach to the process of learning is that of Kolb,
Rubin and McIntyre (1974).

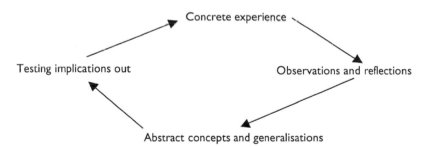

Concrete experience This is simply the part where we do something. We have a go
at handling someone's poor performance, say, or we draft a policy. In terms of
learning, it is important to do this *with as much awareness as we can*. In other
words, we watch what we are doing and store this information.

Observations and reflections We are remembering what happened here on the basis
of our observations and perceptions. We are thinking about the data gathered. For
example, 'When I told him I wasn't happy with his attitude with people on the phone

I noticed he really stiffened up.' This can be about noticing chains of consequences: if you do something in a certain way, something else is likely to happen as a result. We also have to ask: 'Why did she behave in that way with me? Was it because of what I said, or how I said it?' Observation really is the key in this situation – how much can you track what is happening when you are dealing with someone? How much awareness do you have?

Abstract concepts and generalisations We learn to do something differently by developing a model of how one thing follows another in certain conditions. If you understand through reflection and insight, or through feedback, that you tend to talk rather than listen when supervising others, then you will begin to understand their closing down or their dissatisfaction with you.

Testing implications out Learning is about doing, then doing it again differently and better. We want to develop, to improve our performance and that of others. So once we have some kind of model of our behaviour we can modify it, and see what happens.

Case study: mental health project

In a small project working to support young people with mental health difficulties, workers and volunteers had a lot of freedom to work with clients where they found them – on the streets and at two or three recognised meeting places. After several incidents of messages going astray and misunderstandings between staff and clients, and between workers themselves, the project leader started team meetings.

One worker found this very difficult and frustrating, saying with feeling, 'but I want to be out there helping people, not talking about helping them!'

The project leader was able to use the above model of learning to explain that a time of pooling information and perceptions between workers and volunteers could help them as a team build up their knowledge and understanding of their clients so that they could help them more, not less. For example, if workers and volunteers were in clear communication with each other they would be able to prevent confusion and misunderstanding by presenting clear behaviour and policies to their clients. They would be able to discover and share what strategies worked and what didn't when working with particular people.

Exercise: attitidues to learning

(1) Think of three things you remember learning outside of school that are important to you. Choose one of these, and think through the whole process of how you learned it.

● Why did you learn it?
● Who helped you to learn it?
● What was the relationship between you and the other person or people?

- What was the situation?
- Was there anything that made it easier or harder to learn?
- Can you relate your learning process to the adult learning model above?

(2) A second model is useful when planning your approach to conflict and negotiation:

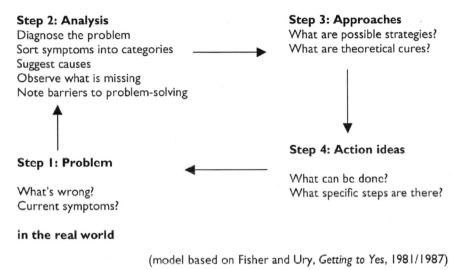

WHAT IS WRONG   **WHAT MIGHT BE DONE**

In theory

Step 2: Analysis   **Step 3: Approaches**
Diagnose the problem   What are possible strategies?
Sort symptoms into categories   What are theoretical cures?
Suggest causes
Observe what is missing
Note barriers to problem-solving

Step 1: Problem   **Step 4: Action ideas**

What's wrong?   What can be done?
Current symptoms?   What specific steps are there?

in the real world

(model based on Fisher and Ury, *Getting to Yes*, 1981/1987)

Case study: carers support project (1)

Mischa is a lone worker for a new, small project set up to support and train carers of people with Alzheimer's. The project has a small management committee that was successful in gaining funding for one worker.

Mischa has worked hard to network with local professionals involved with the care of people with Alzheimer's and has begun a programme of group sessions. What he has found is that once the group gets going it never stops. On the one hand he thinks this might be positive because people are getting their social needs met; on the other he is worried because the group is not addressing its other main aim – to better equip carers with skills.

How can Mischa use the Fisher and Ury thinking model to shed light on his situation?

WHAT IS WRONG	WHAT MIGHT BE DONE

In theory

Step 2: Analysis

The structure for the sessions is unclear

Mischa as group leader is *not leading*

The loudest voices are dominating

People are anxious and needy
Some don't know what should be happening

Step 3: Approaches

Introduce structure – have 'business' before social

Change leadership style to directive

→ Learn group skills

Learn group skills

Step 1: Problem

Mischa feels unhappy with the situation

The group is not meeting one of its aims

He doesn't know for sure if all in the group are satisfied with what they are doing ←

in the real world

Step 4: Action ideas

Go on a group skills training course

Write group members a letter explaining changes to structure and style

See if there are ways to check out people's thoughts and wishes

THE ART OF RELATING TO AND COMMUNICATING WITH OTHERS

'Relationships are an essential resource. They influence our personal happiness, the efficient working of the economy, and the solidarity of the social fabric.' This grand claim is made by the Relationship Foundation – but how does the art of relationship-building break down into manageable elements?

Managers work extensively through verbal communication, and communication skills are essential as they underpin many other activities. However, just as no one likes to think that they are a poor driver, no one likes to think they are a poor communicator. So it makes sense to pay some attention to the skills of communication. Just as we can all benefit from refresher driving skills courses, we can all benefit from going back to the nuts and bolts of effective communication habits.

One-to-one communication

Attending Giving someone our full attention. This is more easily said than done, but is necessary if we are to fulfil a facilitating role with someone.

Observation What are we attending to? What is happening for them? What is their body language saying?

Establishing a context What are we spending time together to do? Clarifying this can be helpful.

Creating rapport All those small things which play such a large part in helping someone feel at ease e.g. offering someone a drink, engaging in small talk to give someone time to settle down.

Active listening

The importance of this skill cannot be over-emphasised. When we are involved in a group and we see someone who is able to get people to participate, who respects others and yet can challenge ideas and stimulate creative discussion, we know that this is precious. Good communication skills are powerful. Asking the right questions is powerful. The fundamental skills of active listening will help discover what they are.

Open questions
'Can you tell me what's happening in the Young People's Drop-in Project?' Such a question enables someone open up and begin the process. It is also useful for exploring new areas and for gathering information. It is not so useful if what you need to do is focus or clarify, or you want someone to talk less for a while.

Closed questions
These are questions that call for 'yes', 'no' or 'don't know' answers. They are useful for checking information and for establishing facts.

Probing or funnelling
'When you said that the meeting went quiet, what happened next? What got it going again?' This approach seeks to go to the next level. 'When you say you felt uncomfortable with the situation, what did you mean?' Here you may be seeking to find out someone's strong feelings or more precise views on something.

Reflecting
This can be helpful to create empathy – the feeling that someone understands what it really feels like for you. 'It sounds like you feel very upset about him leaving.' It may be that you have picked up that someone is upset and want to help him/her to express it if he/she wants to do so.

Empathy
This is about tuning in to what is going on for other people, their thought processes, their attitudes, their feelings about things. If we feel empathy with someone and moreover feel accepted, we will be more likely to open up.

Listening and hearing

This is similar to reflecting, but you are picking up something below the surface that the other person may not yet be aware of saying. Again, being sensitive and tentative can be appropriate; 'I'm getting the impression that when you were talking about freezing in the meeting that was really difficult for you – almost as if you'd done something to be ashamed of. Is that right?'

Checking out

We all make mistakes and jump to conclusions. It is important to check things out with the other person, perhaps through a combination of empathy, reflecting and checking out. You pick something up about someone, then you reflect it back in a tentative way that leaves someone room to say, 'Oh no, that's not what I mean!'

Clarifying

'When you said that you were uncomfortable when the meeting went quiet, was that because you weren't sure what to do?'

Summarising

'Is this right? What you're saying is that when the meeting went quiet you felt panicked, because everyone looked at you for direction and you couldn't think of how to move things on? You froze?'

It may take someone a while to talk something through and get to the nub of it, so it is useful to summarise occasionally to make sure you are on the right track, and that the other person knows you are.

Hypothetical question

This is useful if you want to guide someone in exploring options. For example: 'If you were in a meeting with the team, and a tricky issue came up, let's say about the change in the attendance policy we're introducing, and everyone went quiet, and the atmosphere was uncomfortable, what might you do in that situation?'

Reframing

At certain points you may want to encourage someone to look at something from another point of view: 'Have you considered that you could also have done the following . . .?' This level of skill is advanced, as you have to be sensitive to the possibility that you might meet with disagreement or resistance.

Assertion

Assertion as a set of coherent skills, principles and strategies is essential to personal management competence. (This is drawn partly from *Assertion and How to Train Ourselves*, by Steve Skinner.)

The core principles of assertion are:

- recognising the need to sustain relationships through a balance of rights and responsibilities
- understanding the basic forms of behaviour and their consequences
- developing self-awareness and self-acceptance in order to learn assertive behaviour
- understanding the importance of thinking through how to talk to people in difficult situations.

Rights and responsibilities

These are the starting point for any exploration of assertion. Many voluntary and community organisations are formed out of people's strongly held beliefs that vulnerable or excluded people have rights.

If we think about the Housing For All case study above (page 11), what rights does the director contravene in dealing with his staff in the way that he does? The fundamental right that the director denies to his staff is respect. Treating people with respect means listening to them and acknowledging their contribution to the enterprise and their knowledge, skills and experience. You could also argue that in value led organisations, which often survive and thrive on the basis of people's discretionary effort, staff should have the right to be involved in change and decision-making about change. This is clearly a contentious issue. But not to plan on this basis can mean a tension between a committed staff group who want to be involved and a senior management team who take a more authoritarian approach in their management style, and thus often alienate the very people on whom the organisation depends.

At work, the fact that people work mostly in hierarchical structures means also that line managers have a right accorded to them through their role of giving people feedback. This is clearly appropriate, but what is not appropriate is for this to be done in ways that put down staff and disempower them. Rights and responsibilities go hand in hand. Acting on this principle is very powerful. It will help you stand up for yourself when you feel that your own rights have been contravened, and to treat others fairly when you are the one who is giving unwelcome feedback.

Developing self-awareness and self-acceptance

Thinking about who we are and how we got to be this way can be painful and slow. The key is to acknowledge that we all have feelings and that this is acceptable. Most, if not all, people feel anger or uncertainty at some time. Self-awareness begins with this knowledge – it then moves on to acceptance. Can we accept this? Society puts pressure on us to be in control, to know what we are doing at all times. But recognising our feelings and the effect they have on us and others is empowering. Assertion as a set of principles and behaviour is invaluable in this respect.

Basic forms of behaviour and their consequences

Behaviour	Consequences
Assertive behaviour Valuing yourself and your own feelings Recognising that you have rights and responsibilities Valuing yourself and your own feelings Recognising that you have rights and responsibilities Speaking for yourself ('I think', 'I feel') Developing open, direct communication Practising negotiation Defending the rights of others	This is the *win-win relationship* People know where they are with each other, learn to value self and others, and can go deeper into a fruitful relationship of mutual respect
Aggressive behaviour Angry behaviour involving putdowns, insisting on getting your own way or being right, irrespective of the feelings or rights of others	This is a *win-lose relationship* You may blame others and constantly feel defensive. Others will not feel comfortable with you or respect you for this. Some may retaliate and go to war with you Or people may simply avoid you
Indirectly aggressive behaviour Storing up aggression until someone unconnected with its original source triggers it and you unload the anger on to that person This can also include the manipulation of others	This is a *win-lose relationship* You may avoid conflict with the original person, you may have let off some steam, but you have now upset someone who does not deserve it – and who won't like or respect you for that
Passive behaviour Being sorry for yourself, being over-apologetic and holding back. Feeling that other people are more important	This is a *lose-lose relationship* You can avoid conflict but your self-esteem suffers. Increasing frustration and anxiety. Others may feel sorry for you, or downright annoyed. They will not respect you for passivity

Thinking through how to talk to people in difficult situations

Most workers know they need to plan ahead, to think things through in advance, to call on their experience and knowledge to predict some of the events that will flow from a certain course of action. In the realm of relationships this focus can also be crucial – if we hit a situation where we suddenly recognise that all is not as usual with someone, we should take the time to think it through.

We may find that we are harbouring resentment at the way someone has treated us; those feelings will tend to get in the way of the relationship. Sometimes we may think we can live with this, that we don't need to bring it out into the open. At other times, we just know that we have lost something (trust or liking for the other) and we also know that it is important, in either personal or work terms, to put the matter right.

How do we prepare for this?

Check out your feelings Recognise what the feeling is – unease, confusion, anger, resentment, uncertainty, anxiety. What happened with the other person to bring this feeling about? Was it something he/she said, or the way it was said? If you can get clear on this, you can check how valid your feelings are in relation to the other person.

Once you are clear there is something to say, think about how you will say it. For example: 'When we had that meeting with the Lottery staff I came in late and you laughed – and said I was always late for meetings about money. I felt put down by that in front of people I don't know well. I need them to recognise my professionalism, and your saying that put me on the defensive.'

In this situation we need to refer specifically to the other person's behaviour – what it was that they said or did, and how it affected us.

Listen to the response It may be a mortified apology, it may be a more defensive 'Oh, come on – you're taking it too seriously, I was just joking!' Humour, or supposed humour, can be very tricky. In the above situation you were not laughing, so you may want to press the point in order to see if you can get the other person to acknowledge your feelings, and moreover to recognise the validity of your feelings.

Be prepared for the riposte The other person may take this opportunity to bring up an issue of his/her own. This is not a bad thing as long as you feel that what you have brought up has been dealt with. For you both then to deal with something else is positive.

COMMUNICATION SKILLS IN GROUPS AND TEAMS

The skills of facilitating groups and teams are linked to those of one-to-one communication, and are crucial in all kinds of settings: the teams of staff you directly manage, the multi-disciplinary project or matrix groups you are involved in, and partnership situations.

This material can be read in conjunction with Chapter 3. (This section is largely based on work by Hank Williams in *The Essence of Managing Groups and Teams* and that of Bales's Interaction Process Analysis of the 1950s.) It looks at defining a group's purpose, facilitating groups and meetings management.

Defining a group's purpose

Case study: carers support project (II)

Mischa was employed to develop both support and training for carers of relatives and families with dementia. Having put in the groundwork and encouraged several people to attend on a regular basis, he was having difficulties with how the group sessions went. What he found was that people were talking and sharing with each other enthusiastically but that the sessions never got beyond the more social element. He was feeling frustrated and at a loss.

For different reasons groups take on a life of their own, because this meets their pressing needs, because it is easier than doing something else, because the group need positive leadership. In this situation the worker can call on a range of the skills outlined in this section. Helping the group clarify its purpose is clearly one of them; introducing more structure is another; and using specific communication skills to facilitate this will be essential e.g. being able to interrupt with tact and purpose.

In establishing a structure, group facilitators will need to take into account:

- application of organisational policies
- the context of the group
- individual leadership style.

Application of organisational policies

If a policy exists, it will offer guidelines as to some or all of the following: definition and purpose, contracting, structures, frequency, skills and training, links to appraisal or appraisal-type structures.

Any structure you introduce needs to reflect the policy, as the policy reflects the expectations of the organisation. There are likely to be aspects that are *non-negotiable* by anyone. Others may be *negotiable,* so you need to consider the group's context.

The context and purpose of the group

In the above case study it appears that the support function of the group is working well, but that the second function, that of training, is not. The leader needs to establish direction and guide the discussions so that the second element, training, is addressed. Sometimes it can be a matter of structure or timing. In Mischa's situation it might be better to set aside time for the more formal part at the beginning of the session, with a time limit.

You may be in a partnership arrangement with a number of other organisations from both voluntary and public sectors, meeting regularly as a group to plan and make decisions. This is quite different from formally supervising other staff. However, the core process and facilitation skills remain the same. It is the relationships between the personnel that differ.

Individual leadership style

Are you a directive leader? a consultative leader? or somewhere in between?

Is your tendency to tell or to ask? Do you lead from the front or from behind? This is important in the early stages of setting up structures. If you establish what the organisational or contextual necessities are then you are likely to be left with some room to manoeuvre. Do you then tell your team what will happen or do you open up discussion?

Managing meetings and facilitating groups

Be aware of the difference between task and process. Tasks are *what* you do to achieve your aims or outputs. Process is *how* people do what they do: the ways in which activities are organised, tasks are allocated, people communicate with each other and so on. Process can be more problematic, and it can help to analyse it on four different levels:

Four levels of process in groups

Procedural	How discussion is organised How decisions are made
Structural	Roles in groups, both formal and informal
Behavioural	How 'airtime' is distributed, listening Exploration, co-operation and competition
Social	Dynamics between people, 'climate' Inclusion/exclusion

From top to bottom these processes become more complex and difficult to manage. Why do you need to manage these issues? Because in any group or team situation all four levels of process are in operation and thus affect the group and its performance.

There is overlap between managing meetings and facilitating groups. However, it does help to tease out some distinguishing characteristics. For example, many of the points made about managing meetings apply to any kind of meeting, whereas certain aspects of facilitating groups are more relevant to supervision groups with a focus on learning.

Case study: carers support project (III)

Mischa, the lone worker with this group, has all the above to contend with. On the procedural level, once he has welcomed people the meeting can simply become a free-for-all with no agenda, no clear procedures in place, no scheduled time for training inputs etc. In this context it is the loudest voice that gets heard. Decisions may not get made at all, or, if they are, they will be made by a loud minority.

On the structural level the worker's role needs to be clear, but is not. He has a training role with the group that is not being fulfilled. The role of group facilitator is vague and Mischa does not feel in control of his role.

On the behavioural level he is not enabling those with quieter voices to be heard. It may be that individually some people are expressing themselves, but as a group they are blocked and unable to come to any fruitful discussion or consensus.

On the social level anything could be happening. People often leave groups because they can see no way in which they can participate.

Interactive skills for group-based activities

Group supervisors and meetings managers or facilitators need:

- an understanding of individual and group behaviour
- an awareness of their own behaviour
- an ability to identify causes of problems at the behavioural level of process
- an ability to manage key interactions effectively.

In terms of developing new skills in communication it is useful to bear in mind three issues:

- choices – we do make choices about our behaviour, even if we are not aware of the process involved
- feedback – it is helpful to ask for feedback from trusted people, about specific things, to hear this as perception, and to reflect on it
- practice – we can pick out specific things to practise, choosing the lower-risk areas and attempting only one or two at a time.

There are five key aspects of managing interactions.

Airtime	Who gets it? Who takes it?
Information	How do groups manage the exchange of information?
Ideas	How much are people interested in each other's ideas?
Reactions	How do people react to each other? What is the balance of positive to negative? Are people reacting rationally or emotionally?
Clarity	How is the meeting and discussion structured? What is the true meaning of what people say? What are the outcomes of the discussions and the shared understandings of these?

Airtime

Two key behaviours that underpin the distribution of airtime are interruptions and invitations.

Interruptions can happen too frequently and can be to do with a dominant individual; a competitive relationship; or a chaotic group. However, in some situations there are too few interruptions – perhaps because people are not skilled at interrupting, or because the group lacks energy or engagement.

Case study: carers support project (IV)

Having talked through the situation with a friend (as he has no active line management support available), Mischa has restructured the sessions. He now schedules the more formal business for the beginning of the session and the social side for the second part. He has explained this to the group and they have begun operating in the new way.

All goes well for the first 20 minutes – Mischa outlines behaviour management for people with dementia and then facilitates a group discussion. At this point one of the group launches into a tirade about how useless doctors and social workers are – he has been suffering from the difficult behaviour of his wife for six years and has been given no support whatsoever, and so on.

Mischa realises with a sinking heart that the group member is not going to stop, and he can see that others in the group are getting restless or beginning to start private conversations.

What can he do? At some point, either in this session or the next, he is going to have to use interruption constructively. Once he has done this he will need to follow up by using invitations to involve others.

There are skills involved in interrupting:

- know that you are doing it
- look at the person who is speaking and make eye contact if possible
- if this is not enough, make some kind of gesture indicating 'stop'
- tell people what you're going to do before doing it: 'I'm sorry to interrupt, but I want to tell you . . .'

An invitation is a technique to use to influence the involvement of others. It can ask for the thoughts of individuals and raise awareness of the distribution of airtime. Using invitations can create and protect the contributions of others ('Do you have something you want to add at this stage, Sarah?'). Signal that you want to create a more open climate, put appropriate pressure on someone to contribute ('What do you think, Sarah?') or break up a closed dynamic between two or three people and open up discussion.

Information
Look at how a group manages the exchange of information.

How well is the group managing this at the procedural level? Is the meeting organised so that people who have information to convey are given the opportunity to do so?

How well is the exchange of information being managed at the behavioural level? Are people given space? Are they listened to? Do people ask questions?

What is the balance of telling *vs* asking? Are you someone who does a lot of telling and not much asking? Are you someone who mainly tells and does some asking? Are you someone who asks a lot? The balance of telling and asking affects meetings in relation to:

- involvement: with participation encouraged via invitation and dominance broken down by the asking of questions
- decision-making: for example, by gathering information, evaluating options and testing out possibilities.

Use questions to gather and process information so that decisions can be made; to challenge people to think, think harder and rethink; and to control interactions – we shape what others say and think via questions.

Most people become more effective communicators if they ask more questions. Asking a question focuses on the other person and thus the questioner becomes more aware of that person's needs, and is more likely to be aware of the process of the interaction. Asking questions can help a group to use all its resources; a questioning approach can also generate commitment.

When you ask questions, you signal that you:

- want to involve others – perhaps quiet people

- are interested in what they have to say
- want ideas or opinions from specific people
- want ideas from the group as a whole
- respect their opinions and ideas
- are open-minded and prepared to move position
- are willing to learn from others.

Case study: carers support group (V)

Eventually the day came when Mischa, having again prepared himself, took the plunge and used interruptions to stem the flow from one particular group member. He thanked him for his openness and ability to put his point of view and then declared that it was time to open the discussion out, as others had not yet had an opportunity to put forward their views or describe their experiences.

He looked around the group and asked one of the people who had not yet spoken what her thoughts were.

As people were heading home that evening Mischa went to the person whose views he had solicited and said he hoped she had not felt put on the spot. To his relief the woman said that she was just glad to have been given the encouragement, and that she found talking in groups really difficult, but that if she were never to be able to share her feelings she would feel horribly frustrated. Mischa realised that just as some people need help in stopping, others need help in starting.

Ideas

We can tell a lot about how well a group is working together by looking at how interested people are in each other's ideas. Do people seek them from each other and explore? Do people concentrate on putting forward their own ideas?

Your interpretation of your leadership role will also be important here. Do you feel that it is acceptable for the leader to ask for ideas? Bear in mind the principle that leaders do not have (or even should not have) all the answers. Remember the leadership continuum, and think about where you are on this:

Directive/telling.. Consultative/asking

Ideas are important because they generate energy and create ownership and commitment when participants' ideas are responded to. If, in a group situation, you want to create commitment, it helps to seek proposals – bearing in mind that people have to be able to respond. If people cannot come up with ideas, then, as group leader, you have to propose.

Ideas need development: this means expanding on an idea, progressing it, adding to it or modifying it, yet keeping some essential core. There are three common reasons why the development of ideas doesn't happen:

- the requirement of the meeting is to list options only
- the dynamic may discourage it – it may be competitive/withdrawn
- the skill may not yet be there.

The development or building of ideas is important and affects a group's:

- climate
- teamwork
- ownership and commitment
- quality of decisions.

How can you do more to develop ideas?

- listen to proposals in order to understand them
- evaluate them and your reactions to them
- identify ways in which the idea could be improved
- formulate specific ideas for developing the original idea
- articulate the development in the group.

Case study: carers support group (VI)

Several sessions later the group has moved on. Mischa has restructured the group so the more formal business comes first. This is time-limited, and he reinforces the two central aims for the group regularly. He has had mostly very positive feedback about the change from individuals and the group. Mischa is beginning to feel more confident in himself.

At one group session, in the first part of the meeting, the group is exploring other ways in which carers can be supported and empowered to cope better. A lively discussion takes place as people recount their own experiences, and ideas of how carers could be supported. At one point, when one group member is again describing how he hard he had found it to get help from others, another group member chips in with the idea of getting carers online, so that they could develop a network through email and the Web. Another group member scoffs and says, 'What do we know about this stuff?' The group member with the new idea falls quiet and the discussion moves on.

Not long after, Mischa realises that the idea which had been quietly put forward had not had a fair hearing, and wonders how he can bring attention back to it. Sensitivity to incidents of this sort can be crucial – on the level of reactions, if people feel that others will not listen to them, or take them seriously, they may feel rejected or angry and withdraw.

While building on and developing ideas it is important to be able to find ways to acknowledge people's ideas, and then to explore them, to tap their creativity and energy. Mischa brings the group back to the idea and begins to help them explore it and their attitudes to new technology. It soon appears that some in the group are excited about the possibilities and they decide to have a taster session in order to find out more. By being able to develop ideas through team-building Mischa is having a positive effect on the quality of the discussion in the group, and potentially the commitment and level of participation of its members.

Reactions

We are not often aware of our reacting behaviour. In terms of reacting behaviour in groups we can look for:

- the overall level of reaction: are people signalling their responses to each other?
- the balance of positive/negative reaction
- the nature of the reactions: is it rational or emotional?

Levels of support in a group situation can be affected by how much, and in what way, people agree or disagree in the discussion. These two elements will affect the process of the group interaction, mostly in a rational manner. It is also important to develop awareness of what the *emotional* responses are in the group. There can be a choice in terms of your own behaviour:

- you can *enact* feelings, to express them directly. This can be powerful but is therefore risky
- you can *describe* feelings, to talk about how you, or others, are feeling. This can help create an open climate and can shift the level of the discussion. It can provide an alternative to disagreement and can be used to give feedback.

Clarity

In supervising groups we need to work to ensure clarity, which means paying attention to:

- the structure of the meeting and discussion
- the true meaning of what people say
- the outcomes of discussions and the shared understandings of these.

Here are some examples.

Managing structure by giving *directions*:

- 'Let's start by looking at our workloads.'
- 'Can we go round the group to hear from each of you about that?'

- 'Why don't we move on to some ideas about lightening the load?'
- 'Let's spend some time brainstorming ideas for making this more manageable.'

Getting at the true meaning of what people say by *testing understanding*:

- 'Do you mean that you don't think that any of those will help, or that what Bob was saying isn't going to work?'

Summarising to help achieve better outcomes and shared understandings:

- 'What we've got so far is that everyone is feeling snowed-under with work, but we know that there isn't a way to reduce that in the short term. We've looked at some ideas for reducing the pressure, which I've listed. Some of you can see possibilities in the ideas, but Cath thinks that none of them will make any real difference.'

Key behaviours for facilitating groups

TELLING	ASKING
Giving information	Seeking information
Proposing	Seeking proposals
Suggesting	Seeking options
Building	Seeking reactions
Supporting	Testing understanding
Disagreeing	
Enacting feelings	
Describing feelings	
Giving directions	
Summarising	

Exercise: being and working in groups

Part I

This will help you to identify good practice and your own strengths and weaknesses in facilitating groups. If possible, do it with other staff. Make notes on the questions before finishing and prepare a list of the skills and behaviours of effective group leaders.

- What different groups have you been in, or are you members of?
- What were your experiences of being in this group?
- Positive? How? Why?
- Negative? How? Why?

- What do you think made the difference between the groups that worked and those that didn't?
- What skills and behaviours did the group leaders use?

Part II

Referring to your group's list of effective group leaders' skills and behaviours, spend a few minutes on your own rating yourself in terms of how much, or whether, you do those things yourself.

Make a summary of the list and jot down your thoughts about yourself in relation to each item. Be honest. Rate yourself highly if you believe that to be an accurate reflection of what you do.

When you have summarised the list, rated yourself and jotted down a few comments and examples, get together with one of the group you made the list with and compare notes.

- Can you give examples of where your skills are strongly developed?
- Can you give examples of where your skills are under-developed?
- What can you do to develop your skills in any under-developed areas?

___

Case study: carers support group (VII)

By doing this exercise Mischa was able to see how his experience of groups and his own style of facilitating were developing. He had learned that groups had different needs at different stages of their development. He had discovered that groups sometimes needed a directive style of leadership before they could cope with a more egalitarian style. He had learned a great deal about how and when to intervene in order to move things along.

The results were there to be seen, and felt. The group was positively humming now, and ready for greater things . . .

___

MAKING THE BEST USE OF YOUR LIMITED TIME AND ENERGY

Time is a problem for everyone – or is it? We all know how much time we have for work, and intelligent people ought to be able to work out how much it is reasonable to expect from that time – so why is time management such a fraught issue?

One reason is that it is far from simple to trade off time available against reasonable expectations. All sorts of tensions and dynamics are operating: organisational cultures that govern expectations; individual levels of assertion and unassertiveness, which can make it difficult to set and protect personal boundaries; the demands of new technology; and so on. However, it is still very useful to make an effort to look at our use of time and our expectations of it, because this will help us know whether we are on the right track or not.

If effective management is 'doing the right things well', time management is a personal competence that underpins it.

Given that total control over how we use our time is impossible, it would seem sensible to aim for a reasonable level of control within the context in which you operate. It can help to look at the management role as Rosemary Stewart saw it (in *Managing Today and Tomorrow*):

- demands – the minimum criteria for performance, procedures that cannot be ignored. There may be choice as to 'how'
- constraints – resource limitations, buildings, attitudes and expectations of others (or self). Internal or external
- choices – how the work is done, what work is done.

Consider the structure of your job in these terms. Do the constraints and demands overwhelm and make for very little choice? Is there a lot of choice? What impact can we have on the constraints? It is human nature to enjoy some parts of our work more than others, and to some extent this can be encouraged in ourselves and in those we supervise and support – after all, this will engender motivation. After a certain point, of course, we need to watch that key activities are not being neglected.

How do we make the most of our time? It is about working smarter, not harder. We do this by being ruthless with time and work – but being kind to ourselves and others. It is about changing our habits – and we all know how difficult that can be. The point about being kind to others is important. We know that when we are the victim of someone else's poor time management we pay the price. It puts back our part of the work and things may have to be done more quickly and less well, or we have to work longer hours to do it well because we cannot bear for it to be done in a slipshod manner.

Actively managing time is important, because the feelings of being out of control are stressful, debilitating and counter-productive.

Managing your time

Start by looking at the difficulties you have in managing your time. Difficulties can be anything – something to do with you *or* something to do with other people.

Unless you are a workaholic you have a limited amount of work time. One fundamental principle of time management and management in general is: effectiveness is doing the right things.

Certain areas in most jobs are more critical to the success of the work than others. List the main areas of your job, and to reflect your view of which areas of your job are more critical than others fill in the table opposite. This exercise will help you to identify whether you are spending too much or too little time on any particular activity. You may believe that 20 per cent of your time should be spent supervising staff, but find you are giving this only 5 per cent in practice – and perhaps spending too much time on administration.

Key areas of job	Percentage of total time each should get	Estimated percentage of total time each actually gets

Remember, whereas people who work full-time think of themselves as working 35 hours per week, they do not actually spend this amount of time at their desks.

You may have 35 days' holiday per year . . .

You may go on 10 days' training per year . . .

You may have 5 days' sick leave per year . . .

That's already 50 days away from the coalface. Now you are down to working a four-day week.

Once you are clear about what your key result areas are, it is useful to enter into a planning process. This can involve:

- a 'to do' list
- importance/urgency matrix
- using the matrix to prioritise
- scheduling time.

'To do' list

Take five minutes to write out a list of tasks. Write down things as they come to you, rather than ordering them in any way.

Task or activity		Deadline

Using a 'to do' list is, in itself, a sound starting point for managing time. Yet it will not tell you where to begin. You need to have a method of recognising your use of time and prioritising tasks.

The importance/urgency matrix

High importance	Low importance
Quadrant 1 High importance and high urgency	*Quadrant 3* Low importance and high urgency
Quadrant 2 High Importance and low urgency	*Quadrant 4* Low importance and low urgency

High importance and high urgency	Low importance and high urgency
Quadrant 1 Crises Reactive work Symptoms Stress and loss of control	*Quadrant 3* Interruptions Some phone calls and meetings
High importance and low urgency	**Low importance and low urgency**
Quadrant 2 Planning ahead Creative work Prevention Control and balance	*Quadrant 4* Some phone calls Trivia Escapism Light relief!

When you understand the matrix and the different quadrants take your 'to do' list and transfer each item from the to do list into the appropriate quadrant.

High importance	Low importance
Quadrant 1 High importance and high urgency	*Quadrant 3* Low importance and high urgency
Quadrant 2 High importance and low urgency	*Quadrant 4* Low importance and low urgency

Where are you spending your time? You need to aim to spend time in Quadrant 2. It is easy to get caught in Quadrant 1 – that is, in crisis management.

It is also easy to get side-tracked into Quadrant 3, which again is a reactive position but does not deal so much with key result areas.

Who's got the monkey?

Are you delegating appropriately to your staff, or are they 'delegating' (inappropriately) to you? And are you going along with this? *Management Time: Who's Got the Monkey?*, by William Oncken Jr. and Donald Wass, takes its title from a story about a stressed business manager who walks along the corridor at work and bumps into various of his colleagues. Each time he does so they introduce a problem that needs solving in their work and the boss says, 'Let me think about it and I'll get back to you.' In other words, his staff have delegated their work to him. In the imagery of the story the monkey that needs feeding jumps from their backs and lands on the boss's back. By the end of the day he is groaning with the extra weight and they are leaving the office while he stays behind to solve their problems.

The task in question is to get the monkeys to stay where they belong, with each of the staff, and to enable the staff to feed the monkeys themselves. Think of you and your staff: how many times do you let their monkeys jump from their backs to yours? Be honest. If this happens, you must act. This could mean setting new boundaries, e.g. saying 'Can we talk about this in your next supervision?' and then finding ways to facilitate their development so they can learn new ways of problem-solving.

Case study: family support group

In one organisation volunteers were matched with families experiencing different kinds of difficulties, including children getting into trouble or having behavioural problems. For quite a while the matching process went smoothly and clients reported a high degree of satisfaction and progress.

At one point there were several cases of difficulties between the volunteers and the families. Mostly it was complaints about volunteers not turning up. On the volunteers' side they expressed a feeling of too much being expected of them. This happened at a time when the project was expanding rapidly and the project co-ordinator was snowed under with demands of all kinds. To help him get through such a busy, stressful time he decided to monitor his use of time and see whether this would show him if he was using his own time and energy well or not well. He used the timelog format on page 41 of this book.

Significantly, the co-ordinator found that he was constantly firefighting, reacting to events rather than taking the time to think things through. Furthermore, he realised that whenever anyone had a complaint or problem to address his colleague would always pass this on to him, leaving him to deal with the difficulty and the uncomfortable situations between the volunteer and family.

On the strategic level the co-ordinator realised that he needed to schedule and protect more time for planning and analysis. He also needed to address why his colleague always referred these difficult situations to him. He realised that the colleague just did not know how to handle them, and that this in itself was also problematic. He needed to spend time with his colleague in discussion, in supervision and support. What were his needs?

Planning use of time

Some say that one hour of planning can save 10 hours of work later.

In order to develop Quadrant 2 work we need to bear in mind that to do so usually requires longer chunks of time of time than many managers tend to get. Often the tendency is to move quickly from task to task in much shorter lengths of time. Henry Mintzberg (in *Mintzberg on Management: Inside Our Strange World of Organisations*) tells us: 'Fact: study after study has shown that managers work at an unrelenting pace, that their activities are characterised by brevity, variety and discontinuity, and that they are strongly oriented to action and dislike reflective activities.' Therefore, scheduling or dedicating time becomes essential rather than desirable.

Also, most people have prime and down times. Prime time is simply when we are at our best, our most alert, with our synapses firing and raring to go! When is your best time? Is it, for example, between 7am and 9am, 11am and 1pm, or 5pm and 7pm?

Down time is obviously the flipside of prime time – when when your energy cycle wanes, your blood sugar level plummets and the little grey cells disintegrate. When is this for you? In terms of scheduling you need to dedicate creative work for your prime time and place the tasks that do not need brain power for your down time. Pareto's Law says that 80 per cent of the results we get come from 20 per cent of our activities.

Scheduling time

To do this, use either the weekly schedule sheets that follow or your own diary system if this is suitable. Enter into the schedule time that is already committed. If you have items in Quadrant 1 (high importance and high urgency), schedule these first. If you have crises to manage, you had better make time for them. You may also need to work at getting rid of the monkeys.

Go on from this to begin to develop Quadrant 2 activity (high importance and low urgency) and schedule in the items from this quadrant. You can work back from deadlines, looking at how much time each part of the process is likely to take.

Do not schedule every minute of every day. Perhaps hardest of all, learn to handle your own guilt at not being able to do everything at once or not being able to please others enough.

You need buffer time:

- time between meetings
- time to rest
- time for the unexpected
- time for some things to take longer.

See if you can transfer everything from your matrix sheet to the weekly schedules.

When to schedule time

Daily   Weekly   Monthly   Yearly

For planning and managerial purposes it is important to look to the longer term. This can be done by using planners for the month, the quarter or the year. Thus, if you need to be out and about a lot (for example), you can group together trips to the same locality rather than wasting time by going back to the same area several times in one week.

Weekly schedule

Time	Monday	Tuesday	Wednesday	Tasks
7am				
8am				
9am				
10am				
11am				
12				
1pm				
2pm				
3pm				
4pm				
5pm				
6pm				
7pm				
	Thursday	Friday		Tasks
7am				
8am				
9am				
10am				
11am				
12				
1pm				
2pm				
3pm				
4pm				
5pm				
6pm				
7pm				

Monthly schedule

Monday	Tuesday	Wednesday	Thursday	Friday	Saturday	Sunday

and so on.

Longer-term scheduling

Area	Jan	Feb	Mar	April	May	June	July	Aug	Sept	Oct	Nov	Dec

and so on.

Protecting scheduled time

Everyone knows that we need to schedule time – unfortunately most people find that schedules tend to break down. People make requests or demands, the unexpected happens, things take longer than we expect. If we are to take the issue of time seriously, we must fight to protect what we value by scheduling time.

We can do this by:

- valuing time ourselves
- asserting time's value to others
- asking others to respect this
- establishing clear boundaries and signals
- discussing time and workload management in supervision and team meetings
- using a separate room for quiet work – with a 'Do Not Disturb Unless Urgent' sign
- asking colleagues to cover phones and take messages (screening).

If none of these work, can you negotiate to do thinking work elsewhere?

Also, try to minimise telephone traumas:

- group your outgoing calls
- give others times to ring that suit you
- when leaving messages for someone you wish to talk to, give details of why and suggested times to call you back – this can help to avoid 'telephone tag'.

Organise your paperwork, computer files and email. Research has shown that many workers spend up to two hours a week sifting through the mountain of papers on their desk to find something. In some institutions a mandatory 'clear desk' policy means there must be nothing remaining on desks at the end of the day. How is your desk looking? Aim to clear all piles of unfiled material every three months:

- set aside a decent amount of time – two to three hours
- check that your filing system categories are still valid e.g. files for different activities, subject areas
- if some have changed or become redundant you can change these at the start and as you go along
- start the clear-up: take everything off the desk, shelves etc., and assign every item to the following categories:

File name	Pass on	Throw away	Read	Holding
Once here, they must be put in correct files	To colleagues? Return to sender Delegate	Huge amounts. Be ruthless	On trains When you can't sleep	Things you can't decide on

Repeat every three or four months – this is not a once-and-for-all-time operation. And once you have a clear space, don't let things grow on it. Use the same categories as above for incoming paperwork and email messages, and practise the handle-once-only routine.

If you really want to know how you use your time and energy, use the timelog template following these questions to track what you do and when.

1	What amounts of time were spent on different activities?
2	Does this reflect your key role areas?
3	Which urgency/importance quadrants were you operating in?
4	How was your prime time used?
5	What was the balance between committed and discretionary time?
6	How was your down time used?
7	When did you feel most under stress and why?
8	Did you plan your use of time?
9	What kind of interruptions did you face and how did you respond?
10	Can you see any monkeys you allowed to land on your back?
11	Can you see any situations where you could have delegated to staff?
12	(If you are a manager), what was the balance between managerial and non-managerial work?
13	In retrospect, what could have been done differently (if anything) for the time to have been used most effectively?

Timelog

Time	Day 1	Day 2
7.00		
8.00		
9.00		
10.00		→ etc.
11.00		
12.00		
	↓ etc.	

SURVIVING WHEN THE GOING GETS TOUGH

Some managers like to plan ahead and complete assignments well in advance of the deadlines, whereas others get going only when the deadline looms and the adrenaline cuts in. Which are you?

Each of us has our own preferred styles and habits, with their attendant benefits and risks. The risk of working to the last minute is that it leaves no room for manoeuvre, so it is risky when the stakes are high.

When the going gets tough, what is happening? It could be work mounting up, a personal crisis, an accident, a relationship breakdown, being oppressed or abused at work. Remember:

- when you set up programmes of work, look very hard at what is involved and set a realistic deadline – build in time for the unexpected
- when you work with others, model a way of working based on mutual respect and support: the principle of rights and responsibilities is very powerful
- when you recognise that the going is getting tough, think through the implications – and ask for help. If we have treated others with respect, they are likely to respond in kind and to do what they can to get things back on track
- do what you need to do to build up or refill your reservoir of energy: this will mean different things to different people, perhaps spending some time on your own without having to respond to anybody or anything externally, or connecting up with old friends who were there for you at some time in the past
- be self-aware: many of our problems are self-inflicted in the sense that we don't read the signs, or we read the signs and ignore them
- work, however important it is to us or to our service users, is still only work – it is not everything.

2.

Managing activities

This chapter covers:

- the role of trustees and boards of trustees
- understanding organisations and management
- developing strategic awareness and skill in the planning cycle
- using situation analysis to move forward
- developing cultures and structures that work
- managing change positively
- developing involvement in partnership work.

THE ROLE OF TRUSTEES AND BOARDS OF TRUSTEES

Voluntary organisations and community groups are likely to be one of the following: an unincorporated trust or association; or an incorporated company limited by guarantee; or an industrial or provident society. Section 97 of the Charities Act 1993 defines trustees as the people responsible under the charity's governing document for controlling the management and administration of the charity, regardless of what they are called. NCVO recommends that charities call the people with legal responsibility for the organisation 'trustees' and refer to boards or councils as 'boards of trustees'.

Every trustee should have a copy of the document which defines the organisation's legal status – the governing instrument. If the charity is a trust the governing document is a declaration of trust or a trust deed. If the organisation is an association it will be a constitution. For further detail see *The Good Trustee Guide* (NCVO).

Key responsibilities for boards of trustees

In broad terms, the board's duties are:

- to determine the overall, strategic direction of the organisation, including its mission

- to provide leadership
- to uphold the organisation's financial and other responsibilities under the law
- to nurture the organisation's values
- to develop policies
- to ensure the organisation acts within its charitable objects (purposes)
- to ensure accountability to all stakeholders e.g. the Charity Commission, the Inland Revenue, Customs and Excise, funders, users, staff, volunteers and the public
- to ensure the organisation has sufficient resources for its work
- to ensure that assets are managed properly
- to agree the budget and monitor this accordingly
- to review annually the performance of the board of trustees
- to establish procedures for recruitment, equal opportunities, supervision, support, appraisal, payment of staff and disciplinary matters.

Each board member should have a job or role description. These will vary according to whether or not a board member is an honorary member or not. The honorary members are the Chair, the Vice Chair, the Secretary and the Treasurer.

Individuals have different motivations for becoming trustees — professional interest, personal experience, for example – but all must know what their specific organisational function is so that they can play an active, constructive part. It can help to carry out a *skills audit* of what the charity needs and then to compare the results against the skills and experience of the trustees. This will show who can do what and where the gaps are. It may identify training requirements for the board as well as generating ideas for the kind of people who are needed to fill those gaps.

Priority skills needed by the board

Strategic planning and setting targets
Monitoring and evaluation
Financial management
Knowledge of and ability relating to the kind of work being carried out by the organisation
Legal affairs
Fundraising
Supporting and supervising staff

Further skills useful to the board

Recruitment and selection
Employment law
Marketing and public relations
Information technology
Campaigning

Overall the board needs to be structured properly and clearly. Procedures for meetings and decision-making need to be transparent and accessible in order to ensure fairness and the opportunity to improve the board's effectiveness.

How can busy people with only a limited amount of time make sure all this happens? Boards of trustees should strive towards the *governance* model. Within this model the board should govern – that is, act at the strategic level, while the senior managers should manage. The board should provide strategic leadership, but delegate responsibility to the senior managers to put the strategy into operation, in accordance with the guidelines set out by the board. Also, the board may delegate to sub-boards who will oversee certain aspects of the organisation's operations e.g. a sub-board could be asked to supervise an internal audit.

The relationship between the Chair and the senior manager or chief executive is a pivotal one; the two need to agree on the boundaries of board and management authority. Within the financial framework, for example, how much can the senior manager decide without referring to the Chair or the board? This relationship is also a complex one, where conflicting needs and demands have to be negotiated. It is essential that the Chair supports and supervises the work of the senior manager. Conversely, it is crucial that the senior manager nurtures the Chair and supports that person in his or her role. Their alliance is likely to determine what kind of board emerges.

A colleague, Nick Frost, has drawn up a typology of boards based on his extensive experience of membership of boards and also of chairing them. They are as follows:

The irrelevant board
It meets rarely
Its meetings lack focus
It is ill-informed
It does not have real power
It lacks strategic direction.

The intrusive board
It takes decisions best left to the practitioners
It takes day-to-day decisions
It has too much power
It undermines legitimate professional concerns
It responds reactively – there is no forward thinking.

The effective board
It helps to develop a clear demarcation between the functions of staff, practitioners and board
It sets a clear strategic direction
It monitors and reviews strategy
It accepts legal responsibilities
It supervises and supports managers in their operational work.

Setting up and maintaining an effective board that works along the lines of the governance model can be difficult and needs the investment of time and energy. It helps enormously if the charity is organised in its board development and is welcoming to any new recruits. This means having a clear induction procedure so that new trustees know what the charity does, its structure and history, its current strengths and weaknesses, and above all something of the specific contribution which the new trustee can bring to the work.

The role of the board of trustees is central to the process of setting out the mission and strategic plan, discussed in this chapter.

UNDERSTANDING ORGANISATIONS AND MANAGEMENT

This section sets out some of the theory that has developed in relation to organisations and management, with illustrations from the voluntary and community field.

It sometimes seems that organisational models are developed and then superseded, but elements of many are relevant to understanding different organisations at different moments in their life, structure and behaviour. The source of much of this thinking is the business sector, but it is nevertheless relevant to an understanding of how organisations work.

Scientific management and bureaucracy

Frederick Taylor, in the USA, introduced increases in productive efficiency by questioning traditional work practices and finding 'the best way' each job should be done. 'Taylorism' is a phrase often used to describe factory methods, which fragmented tasks in order to increase efficiency. The danger with such methods is that workers can become bored, disaffected and dehumanised. This is often held to be the root of the problems in the British car industry of the 1960s and '70s – and can be contrasted with the team approach adopted by Toyota, for example.

Taylor also concentrated on developing more sophisticated selection and training methods. Later scientific managers such as Frank and Lillian Gilbreth developed time and motion study, 'with such effectiveness that they were able to increase the number of bricks a man could lay in an hour from 120 to 350'.

But what does this focus on efficiency have to do with the voluntary sector, where people work from a sound value base and from principles of equal opportunities?

Case study: scientific management in the voluntary sector?

A key regional agency had the remit to develop, support and fund a variety of small creative arts projects. Although the budget was large, the timescale was limited and the agency was working under a great deal of pressure. It comprised 12 staff headed by a director and deputy. While the director had a hands-off management style the deputy was left to operate with a highly authoritarian and controlling approach. Her concern was for the work and the need to meet ever-increasing objectives for outputs and productivity. Towards this end she would simply load more and more work on to staff, and when they sought to discuss this she would criticise every aspect of their work performance.

One member of staff sought to challenge both the unfair work demands and the objectionable manner in which she was treated, and received the predictable response – that it was her own shortcomings that were the problem. In the end, realising that the stress of this was affecting her health, she left. For some time after, her self-confidence was severely knocked.

Two years on, she bumped into an ex-colleague who told her that since she had left several others had followed suit; one woman had been on the brink of a breakdown.

The management approach of the deputy director in question may not be a thought-out one, but it is a reflection of an ethos which sees workers as machines – a means to an end. In scientific management it is the managers who think and who tell the workers what to do and how to do it. Just as in this example, there is no room for staff to participate in the thought processes behind the overall pattern and style of the work.

There have been recent examples of ex-staff taking up this kind of issue with their former employers. One such case was that of John Walker, who was awarded £175,000 in an out-of-court settlement from his previous employers, Northumberland County Council. He had had sick leave, which he claimed was due to overwork. This problem was discussed with his line manager and he was promised additional support on his return. This was given at first, then removed. Eventually he suffered a deterioration of his mental health and retired early. The High Court had found against his previous employers, saying that since they had promised additional help, they were aware of his needs and could have foreseen that their employee would be vulnerable if left unsupported.

Obviously, staff are there to perform and to carry out reasonable expectations and requirements. However, the organisational needs can overwhelm the human needs of the workers who are there to deliver the services

The German sociologist Max Weber, known for his analysis of bureaucracy, argued that the market structure of western societies required business organisations to be highly structured, or bureaucratic, with the following qualities:

- clear role definition
- clear hierarchy of authority
- laid-down rules and procedures
- qualification for office
- impartiality.

All of these features still appear in local authority organisations and some larger voluntary organisations and cultures, though with the current modernising local government agenda, driven by the government, substantial changes are on the way. We are all familiar with the feeling that rules can become an end rather than a means. A related danger is that in bureaucratic organisations personal initiative and creativity can be buried. Many voluntary sector managers are worried about the rising levels of bureaucracy that have accompanied the flood of demands for increased monitoring, evaluation and quality assurance on the part of government and funders.

The French engineer Henri Fayol, who took a functional approach to management, concluded that the process of management in any organisation, large or small, public or private, consists of eight basic functions:

1 determining and deciding objectives
2 forecasting
3 planning
4 organising
5 directing
6 co-ordinating
7 controlling
8 communicating.

The main emphasis in this approach is that of rationality. This, of course, is not the whole story and later in the development of organisational thinking researchers began to see other key aspects of organisational importance.

The human relations school

The rational approach always assumed that the objectives of the organisation and individual workers were the same – which is certainly a non-political and non-psychological approach. It was a unitary approach to power in organisations, which takes for granted the right of owners and senior managers to 'govern', on the basis of an assumed shared consensus of interests between owners, senior managers and workers.

Elton Mayo (USA, 1920s) found out, serendipitously, something very interesting. As a researcher he was engaged in exploring the links between rest periods and productivity. This led to some famous work at the Hawthorne Works of the Western Electric Company – which grew into what is called the 'Hawthorne Effect'. The experiments involved changing environmental conditions to see what differential consequences would flow from them. What resulted was an improvement in performance whatever they changed. Hence, they lowered the lighting – performance improved; they raised the lighting – performance improved!

A number of important factors were revealed:

● work pacing is set informally by the group
● recognition of an individual's contribution tends to increase output

- social interaction, especially when controllable, enhances job performance
- grievances – morale is improved by allowing people to air them.

The human relations approach led into the behavioural approach, which delves further into questions of communication (individual and group), motivation and leadership. In a way this kind of research can seem to be very obvious – but at the time it was not. People did not go to work and expect to be *listened to*. The great contribution of this school of thinking is that it places human needs and relations at the centre of organisational life.

Case study: supported housing project

In an independent supported housing project for people with learning difficulties the manager, who had been in post for 15 years, ran a tight ship. The centre of operations was his office, in which he spent almost all his time. Occasionally individual staff would be summoned to be given new directives on how the unit was to be run. No discussion was allowed. On the rare occasion that a new member of staff ventured to challenge him, the answer would always be that the manager knew his own strengths and weaknesses and he was just the way that he was – he could not change.

Although some of the staff would have preferred to work in a different way, others seemed to accept this approach, and all decisions were taken by staff, rather than by clients. Anyone who strongly disagreed with this way of working would fairly soon be ground down and would then leave. The workplace was a quiet place with a sad atmosphere. On the whole, morale was low for both staff and clients.

To everyone's surprise the manager left, and again to most people's surprise the new manager had quite a different approach. They began to have staff meetings to talk about what they did and why. At the same time the new manager began meeting each of the staff individually to get to know them and their work. Eventually, over time, most of the staff realised that this was not some kind of trick or trap, and that the new boss really wanted to work more collectively, as a team. He would praise people for positive work or constructive contributions to discussion, and a new atmosphere and energy began to bubble in the project. Staff even found that they could disagree with the manager and that he would listen – a novel experience for those who had been there for some time.

Staff began to get excited about new ideas, new ways of working and supporting their clients – and, of course, this had, again over time, a very positive response from their client group, who also began to realise that a new kind of relationship was possible.

The point to note is that the way we treat staff will result in very different outcomes – different possibilities and energies will be released.

The learning organisation

This concept has grown in importance in recent years following the impact of globalisation, with its increasing pace of change and growing competitiveness. Peter Senge's definition of the learning organisation is that of a place 'where people continuously expand their capacity to create results they truly desire, where new and expansive patterns of thinking are nurtured, where collective aspiration is set free, and where people are continually learning how to learn together'.

Key principles for the learning organisation are:

- visioning (having a vision) – anyone can do this, irrespective of their position in the hierarchy
- empowerment – whereby staff are enabled to enter into interactive and mutual decision-making
- learning – all staff must be involved in a process of continual learning and improvement. Only continual learning and adaptation will enable organisations to survive, and to thrive.

Exercise: is yours a learning organisation?

On a scale of 1 to 5, how well does your organisation reflect the following learning organisation principles?

1   We regularly monitor the social, political, economic trends that affect us
2   Everyone here plays a part in policy and strategy formation
3   Access to information and databases is as open as possible
4   The financial consequences of actions are fed back to those concerned as soon as they are known
5   Departments and units understand each other's purposes and values
6   There are different ways of rewarding good work – monetary and non-monetary
7   Structures are flexible and change frequently to match needs
8   People bring in and share information about what is happening out there
9   We engage in partnerships to develop new services and to learn
10 People are not blamed for bearing bad news
11 All are encouraged to learn new skills
12 We find new directions by experimenting with new projects
13 Important policies are widely discussed before implementation
14 Information technology really helps us do new things, not just automate the old methods
15 People understand the importance of money and resources, and how these work here
16 Different sections share information and skills, and help each other regularly
17 Most people have a say in the nature and shape of reward systems
18 People are encouraged to come up with different ways of organising work
19 Effective channels of communication exist for collecting and sharing information from outside the organisation

20 We often meet other organisations to share good practice and ideas
21 The focus of our appraisals is the exploration of the individual's learning and development needs
22 Lots of opportunities and resources enable everyone to learn on an open basis.

(based on 'The Learning Company' by Pedler and Aspinall in
The Experience of Managing by Legge, Clegg *et al*, Macmillan, 1999)

How well does your organisation do on these processes?

The concept of the learning organisation stems from a way of looking at organisations which is biological or organic. Biology teaches us about how organisms need to learn to adapt in order to survive in a hostile environment. Similarly, given the rate of change in all sectors, organisations must adapt – or go under. The main lessons of this way of understanding organisational development are:

● to scan your environment and find out what's going on now and what is soon going to happen
● to find out what works in order to survive, and thrive.

Exercise

Global and media concern over environment

Legislation on the environment   Partnership projects with e.g. youth groups

Board of trustees

Department for   New Deal scheme
Education and Skills

Environmental project

Pool of volunteer workers   Other funders

Trends in what draws people to
volunteer

If you map out your own environment in this way it can help you to see the relationships between different parts of the system, see where the influences come from, or are drawn from, see where the problems are, and see where current or future energy needs to be directed and channelled.

Exercise: environmental scanning

This is the kind of exercise to do with a team or board. It is a sense-making exercise, so try to do it with a relevant group of people.

On a large piece of paper draw a symbol for your organisation.
Around it write all the environmental influences you can think of: local, regional, national, international ...

What do all these influences mean to your organisation now?
What might they mean in the near future?
And what could they mean in the far future?

The management role

Another researcher, Henry Mintzberg (1970s), looked at what managers actually did rather than what they 'should' be doing. His approach was descriptive rather than prescriptive. By following and recording what managers actually did throughout the day he found that the following 10 roles, grouped into three areas, were involved in the management task:

Interpersonal roles:

- figurehead – symbolic or representational activities
- leader – directing, motivating, influencing
- liaison – relationships/networking.

Informational roles:

- monitor – collecting formal and informal information
- disseminator – distributing information
- spokesperson – information-sharing outside unit/organisation.

Decision-making roles:

- entrepreneur – working with the environment and adapting the unit to cope; managing change – group and individual
- disturbance handler – reacting to and managing crises; managing in the short term
- resource allocator – distributing resources, both people and materials/finance
- negotiator – interacting vertically with own line management and those managed, and with peers (those on a similar level).

Exercise: your management role

How does what you do fit with Mintzberg's ideas about management roles? This focus can be a useful link to the work on time management in Chapter 1. Knowing how you actually spend your time as a manager is important, as you may be neglecting the very activities that should define your management role.

Where do you spend most, and least, of your time? If it is all disturbance-handling (firefighting or crisis management) rather than leading, you will know that your activities are out of balance.

DEVELOPING STRATEGIC AWARENESS AND SKILL IN THE PLANNING CYCLE

Strategic planning sounds very grand, but isn't. If you go on an important journey, a holiday, for example, you want it to be a success. So what variables are involved in a successful holiday? Destination? Duration? Cost? Who is going and their needs or wishes? Purpose of the holiday (not everyone enjoys the same things)?

It helps to think in the same way when embarking on strategic planning in the workplace. (The best thing about not planning is that failure comes as a complete surprise, and is not preceded by a period of worry and depression!)

Failing to plan = planning to fail. How true is this for you and your organisation?

Why plan?

A starting point is to ask why your organisation is in existence.

Today's climate of uncertainty and rapid change means that organisations cannot stand still if they are to survive (or thrive).

When you have a destination in mind, an idea of the resources to hand and an agreement between the key people, you can move forward confidently and asser-tively ... and with the flexibility to adapt to change. Awareness is essential. The process of planning goes along with the ability to scan the environment: what's happening out there? How is it going to affect us? What do we need to do, and how?

Planning is a potentially integrating activity – given a broad degree of agreement about aims and objectives, a sound plan can bring people together under the same flag.

In this book the term 'strategy' refers to planning for the longer term, rather than the day-to-day operational planning. Day-to-day planning is also crucial, as this chapter will explore later.

It is important to recognise that planning is not clean or scientific, nor is it a once-every-three-years kind of activity. It is about taking a learning perspective on the life of the organisation as a whole. Where is it now? Where are we going to? Why are we bothering? How far along the road are we? Yes, we may have a map to refer to, but no rules as to the stage at which we enter the process. In this sense planning is clearly an incremental process, one that goes forward in stages. And of course, influencing and shaping an organisation involves people, so the process is also political. The different stakeholder groups will want to set course in different directions.

Management and planning

Strategic planning

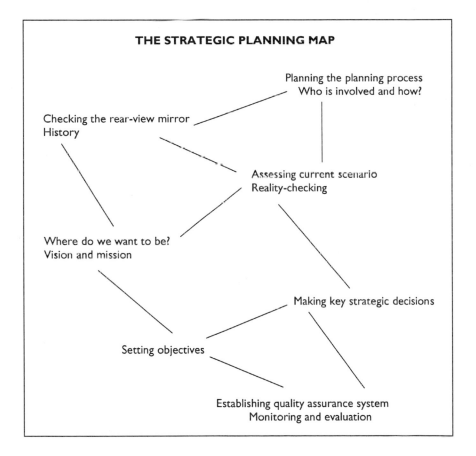

THE STRATEGIC PLANNING MAP

Planning the planning process
Who is involved and how?

Checking the rear-view mirror
History

Assessing current scenario
Reality-checking

Where do we want to be?
Vision and mission

Making key strategic decisions

Setting objectives

Establishing quality assurance system
Monitoring and evaluation

Strategic planning is a process of deciding in advance what to accomplish, and why, and how to go about it. The strategy can be said to emerge from four factors:

1 environmental opportunity – what the organisation might do
2 competence and resources – what the organisation can do

3 interests and desires – what the organisation wants to do
4 responsibility – what the organisation has to do.

The strategic plan will include:

- what the organisation is, its purpose, values and mission
- its aims and objectives
- its main activities and sources of funding
- period covered by the plan
- clear performance measures
- who was involved in drawing up the plan.

Mike Hudson, in *Managing without Profit*, suggests that there are preconditions for strategic planning:

1 Organisations need to have enough independence to be able to select their own aims and objectives. If they are part of a larger system this may be denied
2 There needs to be commitment to the process from senior personnel – chair, chief executive etc.
3 The senior management team needs to be stable
4 There should be a lack of major crises
5 Organisations should distinguish between strategic and operational planning.

These criteria can be used to determine how ready your organisation is to move into the planning cycle.

Business planning

Business planning is a forecast of income and expenditure over a given period. It spells out the implementation of a strategy and shows the feasibility of what is proposed. Business planning is also a way of thinking through different implications for various strategic possibilities. Thus it translates general principles and aims of a strategy into a quantitative forecast of activity and staffing, resources needed and so on (see Chapter 7).

Operational planning

Operational planning is the day-to-day practical planning carried out by everyone in order to make things happen. The broader strategic and policy decisions have been made and day-to-day decision-making should fit within these guidelines.

Planning the planning process

Who is involved in planning and how they are involved is a major issue. Who gets to be involved in decision-making is usually up to those with power in an organisation. The present government is making efforts to ensure, indeed to insist, that organisations such as local authorities, and projects, such as regeneration programmes, genuinely include the community, but putting this into practice can be fraught with difficulties. If we are serious about helping communities to develop, it is vital to consider one of the principles from the Working Statement on Community Development by the Standing Conference for Community Development: 'Community development is about the active involvement of people in the issues that affect their lives. It is a process based on the sharing of power, skills, knowledge and experience.'

It can be helpful to consider three approaches to power and decision-making in collective life in general:

Unitary approach	Pluralist approach	Radical approach
Interests Emphasis on idea organisation being united under a set of common goals	**Interests** Emphasis on diversity of interests; organisation seen as loose coalition of different groups and individuals	**Interests** Emphasis on oppositional class interests; organisation deemed to be battleground where rival groups, e.g. management and unions, fight for achievement of mostly incompatible ends
Conflict Seen as inappropriate and the domain of troublemakers	**Conflict** Seen as inevitable and potentially positive in its capacity to create energy	**Conflict** Regarded as inevitable and also part of a wider class conflict which might eventually change the whole structure of society. Acknowledged that conflict can be suppressed and therefore exist in latent form
Power Largely ignored; concepts such as authority, leadership and control preferred in explaining management's right to manage	**Power** Medium through which conflicts of interest are worked on and resolved. Organisation viewed as plurality of power-holders drawing power from different sources	**Power** Unequally distributed and follows class divisions. Power relations in organisations viewed as reflections of power relations in society as a whole and closely linked to processes of social control, e.g. the economy, legal system, education

(based on Morgan's adaptation of the work of Burrell and Morgan, in *Images of Organisation*)

How does your organisation or system shape up in relation to the above approaches? This is an important question and one that will determine just how much service users, the community and staff are accorded 'rights' to be genuinely involved in the frameworks and structures and processes that affect their own lives.

Exercises to help with planning

What follows is intended to support you in assessing the current scenario from the strategic planning map, checking the feasibility of initiating a certain change, and thinking through the process of implementing and managing the change.

The strategic planning process

We are dealing with complex situations. One organisation may have a vision and mission statement, and may need to review and amend it. Another organisation may not have such a statement, and may need to develop one. Whatever the position, organisations often assess the current state of affairs by using the SWOT approach: strengths, weaknesses, opportunities and threats.

An informal discussion among colleagues might lead to the realisation that there have been significant changes (internal or external), or external pressures, which mean the group needs to review or reposition. The starting point is likely to be information-gathering/situation review followed by clarification of purpose and mission. In the process, it will become clear that planning is not a nice, neat, linear exercise.

USING SITUATION ANALYSIS TO MOVE FORWARD

SWOT analysis

SWOT offers a structure for analysing any area, and provides a foundation for identifying changes needed. The changes can be political, economic, social or technological (PEST).

In order to move forward it is essential to assess and analyse the present, which is what the SWOT tool enables managers to do. It enables analysis of internal and external factors, which could include:

unit philosophy: for example, mission statement	– strategic plans
organisation structure and changes	– admissions policy
departmental policies and procedures	– senior managers
board of trustees	– middle managers
staffing and morale	– conditions of service
training and development	– team culture
resources and funding	– relationship with funders
buildings	– the work you do
equal opportunities	– changing needs
legislative changes	– line management/team leaders
new initiatives or directions	– partnerships with clients
internal communication with other groups.	

Use the pro forma sheet below to generate ideas for the strengths, weaknesses, opportunities and threats as you see them regarding the unit as a whole. It is likely that you will find that certain aspects are multi-faceted: for example, some strengths can also be seen as a weakness, and some threats as an opportunity.

Strengths	Weaknesses
Opportunities	**Threats**

Case study: carers support project (VIII)

After the carers support group has been going for a year it is clear that there is a split in the membership and the board of trustees. There are those who, broadly speaking, see the project as being about support and social contact and those who want to bring about new skills and empowerment for carers. The different groupings within the project want to go in different ways. A new board member on the suggests that they carry out a SWOT exercise together to check the current situation. In the end the exercise is carried out in a session hosted by the board in which group members are invited to take part.

Strengths	Weaknesses
The group provides a great deal of social support for carers It has greatly reduced the isolation of several carers The project has a keen, committed worker whose skills are growing Project members number several that want to play a wider part in moving the project forward	The project is not really addressing its other main aim of training and empowering carers The worker receives no positive supervision and development from the board of trustees It is impossible for one member of staff to do all that needs to be done – she has some gaps in her bank of skills There is no organisational clarity about its place in the world
Opportunities	**Threats**
There are so many more carers out there who are not being helped New legislation around carers means that this is a good time for funding applications New methods of contact and communication are now possible (email/World Wide Web) There is a lot of energy in the group to experiment Reviewing the functioning and purpose of the project seems timely	The split in the group is threatening to hold back, or damage, the integrity of the project: for example, some group members are intimidated by the discussions over different ways forward Loss of support from significant funders if project does not deliver on skills development for carers

This exercise helped the project members begin to realise where the priorities for action lay; they concluded that they had to make strategic decisions in the light of looking again at their vision and mission. This, as they were aware, might also have implications for the structure and functioning of the project as a whole. Also, the issue of a weak board of trustees needed to be addressed.

Exercise: SWOT analysis of your project, group or organisation

Even when you are to go through this process with colleagues it makes good sense to work on your own first, so that you are genuinely thinking for yourself before comparing notes. Once you have done the initial work on your own, work with a partner or, if you are from the same functional area, work as a small group.

Either with your partner or with the small group the aim is to:

- explore your SWOT and develop an overview of the current state of the project or organisation
- think about the priorities for the implementation of possible changes or innovations by yourself
- use your communication skills to facilitate each other's exploration and thinking.

In this process you are:

- drawing on the store of information and opinion you have individually
- drawing on the pool you have collectively – when you work in pairs or groups
- categorising the information and opinion according to a particular conceptual framework
- reviewing any evidence you have for any particular assessment
- drawing out particular implications from your assessments
- drawing conclusions from your assessment and analysis.

This can be a very productive exercise for your team or board. You can assign one of the letters (S/W/O/T) to each of four groups, then get them to focus on that one only and, afterwards, discuss the results.

Checking the rear-view mirror: the road mapping approach

Road mapping is an exercise that explores how people see the progress and development of an organisation or team or service over time. It is particularly useful when it feels as if the group is still carrying baggage from the past or during times of great change. Doing this exercise can be a lot of fun, as people create all kinds of images to match their view of the history of the organisation.

There is no 'must' about using this approach. In some situations it will not seem to be the best use of limited time. Remember, though, that groups can get very much stuck in the past. For example, one organisation had a charismatic director who left and was replaced by someone who took more of a shared approach to managing the enterprise. A lot of time and energy was being used by people, some wishing for a return of the 'old days' and others wanting ever more influence. In going through the road mapping process many of these issues were brought to the surface in a way that people were able to cope with, to discuss meaningfully and to begin to see that it was time for the organisation move on. Also, a great deal of energy was released, often in the form of fun and laughter at the different images and memories.

Exercise: road mapping

Work in groups of no more than eight. Tape together four sheets of flipchart paper to make a large rectangle that gives you enough space. Have pens of different colours.

Pick a timespan to focus on – for example, the past 12 months. The idea is to picture this period for the organisation as a road map.

What comes to mind concerning roads and traffic?

Motorways?
Country lanes?
Roundabouts?
Traffic jams?
Lay-bys?
Lorries?
Motorbikes?
Weather conditions – for example, fog and ice?

When you look back at the start of the period in question, how did the organisation feel and look to you?

Like a Rolls-Royce cruising down the highway?
Like an old banger going round and round the same roundabout?

What has happened between then and now? And how can you picture all this on your road map? Remember, you may see things the same way as others – or you may not. Share perceptions and memories. Discuss them and draw them on to the road map.

Use pictures and symbols. Use different colours – this all makes it more interesting to show others when feedback and discussion are going on.

From establishing vision and mission to setting objectives

It is useful to set out a framework for this process, both in abstract terms and in concrete terms. As managers you need to explain and to help others learn what this process involves, so to strip it down to essentials can help. Thus, in abstract terms:

From vision to time management

VALUES
MISSION STATEMENT/PURPOSE
'What and why'

⇓   ⇓
AIM   AIM

The impact – more specific

⇓   ⇓
OBJECTIVE   OBJECTIVE

'How?' – in general terms

⇓   ⇓
ACTIVITIES   ACTIVITIES

Specific tasks

Case study: carers support project (IX)

Mission/purpose
Io improve the quality of life for carers
of people with Alzheimer's

⇓   ⇓
Aim   Aim

To increase social contact   To develop the skills and
To use new technology to   coping ability of carers
develop a network of carers

⇓   ⇓
Objective   Objective

To run regular programmes   To run skills and
To train carers in the use of   development sessions
new technology   alongside support groups
To train volunteers in
running support groups

Making key strategic decisions

Creating and developing strategy revolves around asking the right questions and making choices. By asking the right questions, we shine a light on what we are doing, why, and how. It is useful to ask questions on the basis of the information gathered and assessed – this may well relate to trends you spot about how the service is working or being used.

Alan Lawrie (in *The Complete Guide to Business and Strategic Planning, for Voluntary Organisations*) urges managers to ask themselves the following:

- is your concern to survive?
- is your concern to consolidate the operation?
- is your concern to diversify, develop or expand?
- should we grow, stay the same size or get smaller?
- should we do more of . . .?
- should we do less of . . .?
- where shall we do it?
- what is our style of work?
- who are our client group(s)? who are not?
- are we a specialist or a generalist service?
- what alliances and relationships do we need to develop?

Remember, the answers to these questions lie in your environmental scan, your situation (SWOT) analysis and your collective (or individual) interpretation of these. What we are doing is, as always, seeking to discover what the powerful questions are.

Quality assurance: monitoring and evaluation

Quality, which has become such a major issues in the development of organisations in recent years, is covered in some detail in Chapter 4.

CULTURES AND STRUCTURES THAT WORK

The concepts of culture and structure become interwoven in organisations and it may be hard to separate them.

The word 'structure' conjures up ideas of 'shape' and the relationship between different roles and rankings in organisations, the way that power is distributed within the hierarchy. Not all organisations are structured as hierarchies, of course; there are collectives based on consensus and there are co-operatives formed as democracies. However, as we well know, most organisations are formed as hierarchies or pyramids of power and responsibility.

Culture is about 'atmosphere', or 'the way things happen around here', a combination of visible and invisible variables. Some managers, it has been suggested, like to think of it in terms of their organisation's personality – the values, ideas and rules that lead to certain modes of behaviour and group organisation. Culture is made up of 'an organisation's shared assumptions. These create a way of thinking, feeling and behaving that gets passed from group member to group member and permeates the way the work gets done. It is the parts of an organisation that are almost taken for granted.' (*The Toolkit for Managers* by Tim Pickles and Penny Sharland)

Structure is seen to be influential in creating culture. A glance at the various initiatives in organisation development shows that the trend has been toward breaking down or breaking up over-formalised bureaucracies, which are seen to stifle innovation, creativity and flexibility, and to create smaller, more independent units that can self-manage according to guiding principles and values from the core of the organisation.

Case study: community-led playgroup

The interweaving of culture and structure in a small community-led playgroup

formal board of trustees

⇓

⇓

⇓

playgroup manager

⇓   ⇓   ⇓   ⇓   ⇓   ⇓   ⇓
four playworkers   student   cook   part-time administrator

On paper there is a clear structure of authority – the chairperson leads the board of trustees which supervises the work overall and manages the manager who manages the rest of the staff. It sounds reasonable, and looks fine on paper. But in reality it might not work like this at all. The actual workings of this organisation might be like this:

part-time administrator

⇓

⇓   ⇓
disorganised board   weak manager

⇓ ⇓ ⇓ ⇓ ⇓ ⇓ ⇓
rest of staff

What we have to take into account, again, is the impact of personality. In this situation both the manager and the board were weak or undeveloped, which created a sort of vacuum. Vacuums tend to get filled, and in organisational structure the likelihood is that a strong personality will step in – as happened with this playgroup. Here, there was an atmosphere of disorganisation at the top, a staff group who could not look to their manager for guidance or support, and a large vacuum that a part-time administrator with a strong personality, and a finger on the fundraising pulse, could effectively take over.

Exercise: learning about culture in your organisation

Part I

Think of two places you have worked in that have had very different cultures. Describe the two in terms of atmosphere, feelings, dynamics, rules and norms. Try to tease out what made these two cultures the way they were.

It has been suggested that culture manifests itself in organisations at three levels:

- artefacts – the visible level of organisational structures and processes, including all that we see on the surface, buildings and layout, the way people dress, the known myths and legends people talk about
- espoused values – strategies, goals and formal philosophies, day-to-day operating principles that are spoken about, for example
- basic underlying assumptions – unconscious, taken-for-granted assumptions, beliefs, perceptions, thoughts and feelings.

The third is the deepest level of culture and is embedded in the organisation, not confronted or debated ('We've always done it this way').

Part II

See how you can apply the above ideas of culture to the two examples you picked for Part I.

Structure in organisations

'Structure is the pattern of relationships among positions in the organisation and among members of the organisation. The purpose of structure is the division of work among members of the organisation, and the co-ordination of their activities so they are directed towards achieving the goals and objectives of the organisation. The structure defines tasks and responsibilities, work roles and relationships, and channels of communication.' (Laurie Mullins, *Management and Organisational Behaviour*)

'Good organisation structure does not by itself produce good performance. But a poor organisational structure makes good performance impossible, no matter how good the individual managers may be. To improve organisation structure . . . will therefore always improve performance.' (Drucker quoted in Mullins' *Management and Organisational Behaviour*, as above)

When thinking about how you might structure a project or organisation, it could help to take into account the following issues of structure as highlighted by Mullins.

People – organisation relationship
⇩
Clarification of objectives
How will the work be divided? What groupings of staff will there be?
Centralisation and decentralisation – how much power will reside where?
Span of control – how many staff will each manager be expected to supervise directly?
Scalar chain – how many levels in the hierarchy will be useful?
Formal organisational relationships
Will there be project or matrix groups drawn from different sections?
⇩
Maintain the balance of the socio-technical system
and effectiveness of the organisation as a whole

'Socio-technical system' means the people–organisation relationship, which needs to be thought through. An organisation is not just a structure filled by roles, nor is it just people doing their best: the people and system are interacting with each other.

Exercise: learning about structure in your organisation

Draw the structure for your organisation, including boards or board of trustees, if relevant. Does the structure work? What issues arise concerning the structure and the roles, and the personalities who fill the varying posts?

What issues of culture arise from the organisation's structure?

MANAGING CHANGE POSITIVELY

Both the public and voluntary sectors are having to learn to deal with many layers of change, and to accept that change is a never-ending process. The government enacts new legislation, makes changes in funding structures and opportunities, expects increasing levels of consultation and partnership – and each time the voluntary sector must respond to and absorb the changes. At the local government level shifts in relationship and funding changes impact on the voluntary sector. The expectation that the voluntary sector should become more and more professional (e.g. by adopting quality systems) adds to the pressure for change and improvement. Trustees and managers must manage these changes as best they can.

Change is never easy, and is often stressful. Rapid, unwelcome change is inordinately upsetting, whatever sector one works in. What follows should help managers to manage change in ways that keep people on board rather than alienating them.

The change process

In acting as a change agent, as an initiator of change, the following areas will need to be addressed:

- recognition of the need to change
- assessing feasibility
- mapping and planning out the change/'unfreezing'
- implementation/changing
- consolidation/'refreezing'.

Recognition of the need to change

Whether you want to or have to introduce change you are likely to act as a change agent at some point. It may be that you are directed to make changes. It may be that as part of a situation review you recognise that part of the work can be improved through changing some aspect of it. The process of going through a strategic planning process can throw up directions for change. Using the SWOT analysis is an excellent way of identifying the areas that need working on. The SWOT/PEST approach is likely to reveal key questions, assumptions, doubts, conclusions and insights relating to your area of operation.

Assessing feasibility

Change is never clear-cut or neat, and it is certainly true that the ability to tolerate ambiguity and uncertainty is very useful to managers. We know when we reflect on ourselves and on our organisations that we mostly operate within a 'comfort zone' and that leaving this can be painful. A framework for change that both recognises this and moves beyond it is that of Kurt Lewin, who was very interested in the work of groups. He offered a three-phase framework:

(1) Unfreezing

This is the stage when the need to change is recognised. It could be that a worry emerged gradually, or there could be a sudden major threat, or a review process may have revealed that a new direction should be taken. Clearly, change comes from without, as it comes from within, at an organisational level, at a departmental level, at an individual level. If change arouses strong feelings, an act of containment may be necessary to 'hold' the range of feelings of others. Working constructively with such feelings can help people to come to terms with the realities of the changes to come, and thus forms part of the unfreezing stage.

(2) Changing

Making the changes happen – implementing change – comes next. Key considerations are the approach to implementation, how power is used, how people are involved, and how decisions are taken and groups and individuals are managed.

(3) Refreezing

This is about consolidating the change, establishing new routines and rebuilding stability. It may be that the change does not take root and the refreezing simply refreezes the old pattern. Otherwise, it will be that gradually the new ways are incorporated into the fabric or culture of the organisation.

Assessing feasibility using Lewin's Force Field Analysis

Before attempting to plan change strategy, try to assess how realistic it is to take your idea forward. Using Lewin's Force Field Analysis you will be able to assess the feasibility of your idea. Lewin argued that in many situations there is a point of equilibrium. If the situation is stable it is because the 'forces' inhibiting change are equal to the 'forces' that seek to drive change. It helps to see this in a diagram:

Driving forces	Restraining forces
→→ →→→→ →→→→ →	⟨ ←←← ←
⇒⇒⇒⇒⇒	⇐←←⇐←⇐←←
→→→→→→	←←←←←←←

The types of forces that might be involved include:

personal	– ambition, fears, personal agenda, different personalities
values	– a recognition that an existing situation is unfair
interpersonal	– allies, sub-groupings as in political alliances
inter-group	– conflicts or co-operation between sub-systems
organisational	– e.g. a new focus on cost or income, a move towards a restructuring of hierarchy and power relations
technological	– e.g. new technology, new computer systems
environmental	– new legislation may exert a new pressure on the situation.

Case study: carers support project (X)

The reviewing process for the carers support project came from the realisation by the worker, Mischa, that there was a split in the membership between those who wanted the project to have a support-only function, and those who wanted it to be more. As part of their discussions towards clarifying their vision and mission, and their aims and objectives, they carried out a force field analysis based on the question: 'Should the project stay as it is or restructure to broaden its aims and objectives?'

Driving forces	Restraining forces
A worker who is alive to new possibilities ⇒ ⇒ ⇒	⇐ ⇐ Project members who want it to stay the same
Several project members who are excited about new technology →→→→	←←←←← A still relatively inexperienced worker
A board of trustees waking up to its responsibilities to govern →→→	←←← Anxiety about alienating members
→→ The timing – new legislation and funding possibilities	←←← The realisation that the board of trustees is also relatively disengaged
→→→ The fact that there are so many more people to help out there	
→→→ The fact that the project is not fulfilling one of its own aims – the skills and development one	

The conclusion for the vast majority involved in the process was that there were more driving factors, and that the energy for progress and development was so strong it probably could not be stopped. At the same time it was acknowledged that the core function of the support sessions had to be recognised and protected for all those for whom this was the main point of being a member.

Working on the situation in this way can reveal what is involved – culture, structure, values and so on. What you can then do is to explore and identify where you need to place your focus and find the leverage necessary to make the shift, if indeed you decide to go ahead, as they did in the above example.

Exercise: create a force field

Create a force field to illustrate your situation for change. What can you see that might drive your change, and what hold it back? Having done this, can you identify any ways the driving forces can be strengthened? Can you see any ways that the restraining forces can be reduced? In other words, can you see any ways to shift the balance in favour of change?

Draw up a force field to illustrate your situation.

Does it look as if there are levers to work on to bring the desired or necessary change about?

Driving forces			Restraining forces
$\Rightarrow$	Personal?	$\Leftarrow$	
$\Rightarrow$	Values?	$\Leftarrow$	
$\Rightarrow$	Interpersonal?	$\Leftarrow$	
$\Rightarrow$	Culture?	$\Leftarrow$	
$\Rightarrow$	Organisational?	$\Leftarrow$	
$\Rightarrow$	Structural?	$\Leftarrow$	
$\Rightarrow$	Environmental?	$\Leftarrow$	
$\Rightarrow$	Inter-group?	$\Leftarrow$	
$\Rightarrow$	Technological?	$\Leftarrow$	

Mapping and planning change

Remember, particularly at this stage, that change is often difficult for people. Also, bear in mind the difference between being the 'driver' and the 'passenger'.

Exercise: resistance to change and how to overcome it

Look at this list of reasons why staff resist change. How many can you relate to an organisational change you have experienced?

1   loss of control
2   excess uncertainty
3   the surprise effect
4   the difference effect – having to brave life outside our comfort zone
5   loss of face
6   worry about competence
7   ripple effects
8   more work
9   past resentments
10 the threat is real!

The following are ways in which managers can build commitment to change:

1   allow participation in planning
2   leave choices within the decided
3   provide a clear vision
4   share information fully
5   divide large into small steps
6   minimise surprises
7   allow digestion time
8   demonstrate own commitment
9   make standards clear
10 give positive reinforcement
11 reward pioneers and innovators
12 support staff in finding extra time and energy
13 avoid creating obvious losers – if there are some, be honest about it
14 allow mourning the past.

(from 'Managing the Human Side of Change' by Rosabeth Moss Kanter, in Management Review,
April 1985)

Involvement, commitment and opposition

Managers operate with varying motivations and pressures. Some will want to work with others in a joint approach (some will not), and some may have external driving pressures regarding speed. What needs to be found is the fit between your preferred approach and whatever constraints are in place.

Mapping key people

One approach is to map out the key players in a way that shows their relative positions to the change according to a set of possible roles (from *Mapping Change and Innovation*, by Gerry Smale):

- innovators or change agents – those who actually introduce something
- early adopters – those who are keen to learn and develop, strong networkers
- uncommitted.

Other roles are:

- product champions – those who are early adopters and who spread the message
- gatekeepers – those who control resources needed by the organisation
- opponents – those who are hostile to the change or innovation.

In the context of our case study on the carers support project, we can see the players involved in the project and its review in terms of their positions on the possible change of direction for the project.

Example from carers support project

Worker   Project members A, B, C = opponents

= innovator

recent trustee board member
= champion

Project members D to J = not committed

project members K to P = product champions

funder representative = champion

By using the mapping approach you can begin to see who stands where and also whom you need to encourage to move to a new position. Other questions to consider may be:

what does the change mean to the different players?
does the change alter their identity in some way?

Sometimes change is labelled as first order change, sometimes as second order change. First order change lies within the existing pattern of relationships and roles. Second order change indicates a change in the rules – the nature of the system – significantly altering the patterns of roles and relationships. Clearly, people's reactions will be the stronger if the change is second order.

Are they active or passive in the process so far?
Do they perceive themselves to win or to lose in the process?

Through the above process you can move on from the force field analysis to a more detailed analysis of the situation, where it becomes more apparent who you need to work with in order to bring the change into being. This will lead into ideas of how to begin to make the shifts happen, for example, by bringing together product champions and early adopters.

Five approaches to implementing change

(After Thurley and Wirdenius, 1973, adapted in the Open University 1997, and Smale, op. cit.)

Mapping yields a lot of information about the system you want to influence. But how are you likely to go about it?

(1) The directive approach
This is 'management's right to manage change'. Change is imposed and others are not involved in the process. An advantage can be speed but clearly there can be many

disadvantages of the kind outlined by Kanter above. To succeed, directive strategies are likely to need strong personal and position power, the possession of relevant information and an ability to overcome the inevitable resistance. Ruthlessness may be essential.

(2) The expert approach

This can be adopted when the problem is seen as a technical one that needs solving by experts. Here questions may focus on whether the change, for example, the introduction of a new information system, is objectively in the best interests of the organisation. Advantages may be that expertise can be applied, and that a small project team can introduce change quickly. However, others may not see the problem as technical and may therefore be resistant to the proposed solution.

(3) The negotiating approach

It may be recognised that staff should have a say. In second order change, it may be necessary to renegotiate roles and responsibilities. Where staff have some power to oppose change, this approach may be the wise one. Clearly, a potential advantage is that if both or all parties have won a little, they will give their commitment. This approach takes time.

(4) The educative or normative approach

The emphasis here is on winning hearts and minds through organisation development activities and others. These could be consciousness-raising (conferences with opinion leaders and product champions), training in specific skills, team-building work, workshops on inter-disciplinary working, reorganisation and development of inter-group relations. There is also scope for work through the usual framework of staff supervision and team meetings. Again, the advantage is in greater commitment. Time, once more, is an issue, as is the need to devote resources to this approach.

(5) The participative approach

A key assumption behind this is that people will not commit unless they have involvement. With this approach change could be led by a representative group of staff, or the whole staff if numbers permit. An opportunity arises for a rich and creative organisational process here – truly belonging to the learning organisation. Once more, the disadvantages are pressures on time and resources.

Case study: carers support project (XI)

It was soon apparent that implementing the changes at the carers support project would require a mix of approaches. It seemed essential to begin with a participative approach to build consensus to move forward. This was achieved. Thereafter, other approaches also became relevant.

Given the mandate gained through the joint decision-making process from the review, a directive approach with negotiating elements was adopted in order to structure group sessions in new ways. Some sessions were to be based predominantly on support, others on skill-building and development. The fact that this was to happen was not negotiated but once the new structure was in place members could negotiate over how their particular sessions were to be run and managed. Once the new structures were in place, a highly participative culture was fostered by an enabling leadership approach from group facilitators.

At the governance level the board gained enormously in confidence and skill and continued to be engaged in steering the project's overall direction, purpose and development.

Exercise: plan your own strategy for change

A situation review (SWOT analysis) led to assessing feasibility (force field analysis). Now, map out your own system and to plan your own strategy for the implementation of change. Again, it can be useful to begin this process on your own, then talk it through with someone to test out how it sounds.

Implementation

Keep the following in mind:

- put into effect the detailed strategy arising out of the framework of mapping and planning – this will involve a lot of communication
- do more of what works
- work with allies
- listen to the feedback
- if you are getting negative feedback, can you alter the way the change is introduced? Can you change your own behaviour? Are you communicating clearly?
- try to act as a role model.

Some of Kanter's points on how managers can build commitment to change (see page 70) apply here.

Consolidation

This is the part when refreezing, as in Lewin's model, occurs. The change ceases to be new and through a process of reinforcement (carried out initially in implementation) it merges within the system. It can be sensed at this point that something is moving from being a live issue to being part of the scenery.

By now you can see what the consequences of the change have been, whether the problem has been solved by the change and whether there have been any unforeseen consequences of the change. And through monitoring and review you may be already planning new changes. For an example of successful innovation Smale points to the community social work innovators of the 1980s and describes certain key elements:

- innovators held clear, shared principles – they worked with a strong vision and mission
- they worked actively to apply these values in whatever they did – in active problem-solving ways – thus constantly changing practice and approach.

In relation to the 'adoptability' of change it helps if all or most of the following conditions apply:

- there should be enthusiasts or product champions
- there should be no conflict with current national or organisational policies or established climates of opinion among professionals and other groupings
- the innovations need to have local appeal to those who have power to promote change
- the innovations must meet the perceived needs of clients or staff, and not require major role or attitude changes
- the innovations should be adaptable to local circumstances
- little finance or other resource should be required.

Given that our attention is rightfully on thinking through how putting others through change can be done well (that is, it works for the organisation, the clients and the staff), it is worth recalling our own experiences of being put through change.

Case study: Housing For All (II)

Since the meeting between the director and the Troubled Trio (page 12), which ended in a spiral of increased defensiveness and aggression by the director, things have gone rapidly downhill.

Not only did the director not ease off but he tightened up more, perhaps in a vain effort to shore up his disappearing credibility. This led to a soup of discontent and anger. Several staff members have taken out grievance procedures against the director, the work of the service is now suffering and more and more clients are complaining because the staff are behind with their work or are treating the users with less than the customary patience and respect. Finally the board of trustees, having woken up to the fact that the organisation is falling apart, is holding emergency sessions to discuss what to do.

Some of the board have come down in favour of sacking the director. Others, the majority, have argued that he has given a great deal to the organisation and clients and that it is their responsibility to mount a rescue operation.

The board of trustees has yet to decide on a plan of action, but it does recognise that there must be change, and soon, if the whole organisation is not to lose its credibility. The board has included the director in some of the emergency sessions and together they are attempting to thrash out both explanations and ways forward.

Exercise: assessing the situation in the case study

Make an initial assessment of the situation. What comes to mind as an explanation for the turn of events?

What key factors are involved? Is organisational structure a factor, and, if so, how?

What planned strategies for change can you think of, and how might these be implemented?

Analysing the case study

An initial assessment shows how isolated the director is – he seems to be the only one without a reference group. Now, given his personality and style, he would not find it easy to create one for himself, but this puts the onus where it should be – on the board of trustees.

Part of this problem falls into the classic syndrome of the isolated and unsupervised manager. This is a common situation in the voluntary sector, reflecting a failing on the part of the board to ensure that the senior manager's needs are met, and of the senior manager who has not campaigned to ensure that his needs are met – whether through the Chair, or external non-managerial supervision, or mentoring.

As the pace of change has heated up and caused added pressures on the organisation, these have been mirrored by the director on to the staff and procedures, in what seems to be a highly punitive way. What has been lost is any sense of the achievements and skills of the staff and the organisation as a whole.

Changes have been forced on to the organisation which have weakened individual staff members' sense of control. This is threatening, and makes some more defensive or aggressive in their actions and behaviour.

What key factors are involved, and how?

History – this needs some reflection so that the chain of events can be unpicked. The road mapping exercise could help, but would probably need to be facilitated by a consultant.

Culture – organisations such as Housing For All thrive because people with strong social values work hard in them. Unfortunately, as the organisation has grown the formal culture has become too bureaucratic and is stifling, if not punishing, people. A negative culture has been created and is being sustained.

Structure – the director is sandwiched between the (until now) hands-off board of trustees and the staff group. He needs to be supported and guided by the board (or through non-managerial supervision from an external person) and perhaps, in addition, a deputy post needs to be created so that there is a management duo instead of a sole leader.

Participation and involvement – the voluntary sector is a value-driven sector. Staff expect to be consulted, and listened to, and this is not happening.

Planned strategies for change

Create a forum in which people can talk about how things have changed, what they miss and what they are good at within the organisation. For this organisation support for the director needs to be built in so that this can happen constructively. At the forum, set clear ground rules about listening and respect.

Create support structures for the director: this could be a short-term measure, for example, board representatives being there for his support; or it could be long-term – for example, setting up a deputy post.

Create other forums within which staff are involved in discussion and decision-making over defined aspects of the change process. This could include a collective SWOT analysis as this exercise focuses on all relevant aspects of organisational life – positively as well as critically.

Set up regular meetings between director, board of trustees representatives and team leaders. The team leaders are a prized asset and should be nurtured.

Re-focus the culture within the supervision sessions and structures to represent a genuine philosophy of development and appraisal, not punishment.

DEVELOPING INVOLVEMENT IN PARTNERSHIP WORK

Key elements

More and more the voluntary and community sector works in partnership – partnership with other voluntary and community groupings and partnership with organisations from the public and private sectors. The following is based on a resource designed to support voluntary and community groups assessing what is needed for successful cross-sector partnerships. It begins with a formula:

shared goals + mutual advantage + teamwork approach = something greater than the sum of the parts.

All of this depends on the following:

- trust and openness
- joint responsibilities
- problem-solving
- learning and continuous improvement

– which need to be demonstrated over the medium to long term.

You can explore the overall formula by working through this checklist in relation to a partnership you are involved with:

Shared goals

Is there enough common ground and sense of what the parties want to achieve together? This doesn't mean having the same set of goals. Partnerships are characterised by the coming-together of different interests. Tensions and conflicts are inevitable, but the jockeying for position can also be a very positive part of the process.

Mutual advantage

Is each party clear and confident about the benefits of the partnership from its own perspective?

There must be gains that match in some way the investment of time and resources. Individual organisational benefits to be gained might include:

- achieving organisational objectives
- attracting resources
- gaining respect and recognition
- satisfying the requirements of various stakeholders.

Teamwork approach

Are people carrying out partnership tasks as a team, with clearly defined responsibilities, using the best mix of complementary skills and resources?

Partnerships are about organisations and people working together towards common goals, not just networking. A team approach should start from an assessment of what participants want to achieve and what the respective strengths are. In this case some of the strategic planning and change management methods described above will be useful.

Success factors

Trust and openness

Do partners carry out their relationships in an open manner, aiming to build mutual trust and respect?

Key elements for building trust within relationships are:

- credibility – doing what you say you will do
- competence – doing these tasks well
- showing respect and giving credit to others
- openness – about how you work or about the difficulties along the way
- active listening to others and encouraging their participation.

As it helps in team-building events to establish ground rules for participation, so it can also help in establishing partnership working.

Joint responsibility and accountability

Do partners share responsibility for the success of the work and are they accountable to each other for their contribution?

It is important to have a planned and organised approach to the work: how will success be measured?

Problem-solving

Do partners approach problems constructively to find and develop solutions?

In some cases there can be a culture of blame (which achieves nothing) when things go wrong, rather than an emphasis on what can be done to put things right. Remember, you want win-win situations, not win-lose (let alone lose–lose) ones.

Learning and continuous improvement

Do partners actively seek to learn from their work together, to improve their individual and collective abilities?

The process of working in a partnership matters – the results are more than the sum of the parts. The quality of the achievement is vital (see Chapter 4), and time should be set aside to assess how well the partnership is doing, and how it is doing it, with a view to constant improvement.

The medium to long term

Do partners view their commitment to the partnership as one that will live over the medium to long term?

If this is not the case, there may be too few perceived rewards for individual partners to make the significant commitments needed to sustain the partnership approach.

Working in partnership brings much of the core activities of both managing organisations and managing people together. The glue is the central competences which will bring to life what you have learned about already – communication and relationship-building, assertion, working in groups with a team development approach, and so on.

3.

Managing people

Managing people is something that is often left to chance. This works when things go well but can be catastrophic when things go badly. Trustees and senior staff need to know about the relevant employment legislation – both to protect the organisation and its work and also to make sure that the rights of people in work are upheld. And there is a lot of legislation to take into account: Equal Pay Act 1970, Rehabilitation of Offenders Act 1974, Sex Discrimination Act 1975, Race Relations Act 1976, Disability Discrimination Act 1995, Trade Union Reform and Employment Rights Act 1993, Employment Rights Act 1996, Asylum and Immigration Act 1996, Police Act 1997, Working Time Regulations 1998, National Minimum Wage Regulations 1998, Human Rights Act 1998, Criminal Justice and Court Services Act 2000, Care Standards Act 2000, Maternity and Parental Leave (Amendment) Regulations 2001 and so on.

If this list of legislation is intimidating then perhaps it is time to act yourself and make sure you know where your organisation is operating within the law and where it may not be. A recent survey carried out by Ian Cunningham at Strathclyde University has found that 24 per cent of charities had undergone an industrial tribunal in the preceding year. This compared to about 12 per cent for other types of employers. The survey found that problems exist particularly in smaller charities and larger, non-unionised ones which have grown rapidly in employee numbers. This book cannot explore the legislation in detail – books and resources specifically for this purpose are listed in Further Reading and Resources. Rather, it aims to set out frameworks and guidelines for achieving best practice in managing people.

A useful guide to good practice in relation to employee equality is the ten-point plan produced by the Commission for Racial Equality:

1 Develop an equal opportunities policy that covers recruitment, training and promotion
2 Set an action plan, with targets, so the organisation and staff know what can be achieved

3   Provide training for everyone, including managers, so they understand the importance of equal opportunities. Provide extra training for those who recruit, select and train staff
4   Assess your present position (using a SWOT perhaps – see Chapter 2) and establish the starting point for action
5   Review recruitment, selection, promotion and training procedures regularly so you know you are achieving the policy objectives
6   Draw up clear and justifiable job criteria – which must be job-related
7   Offer pre-employment training where appropriate, to prepare job applicants for selection tests and interviews. Consider positive action to help ethnic minority employees to apply for jobs where they are underrepresented
8   Think about your organisation's image: do you encourage applications from underrepresented groups? Do you represent women, ethnic minority staff and people with disabilities in recruitment literature?
9   Consider flexible working arrangements, career breaks, and providing childcare in order to support women and parents so that they can both work and meet their domestic responsibilities. Consider providing special equipment and support for those people with disabilities
10 Develop links with local community groups, organisations and schools in order to reach a wider pool of potential applicants.

The management of people, as distinct from activities, is a crucial function whatever sector we work in, but perhaps especially important in the voluntary sector, where money alone is rarely the prime motivator of the workforce. This chapter covers the essential areas of people management in terms of structures and skills:

● staff and volunteer supervision and support, with a supervision and appraisal model
● managing poor performance
● developing teams that work together and well.

THE IMPORTANCE OF STAFF SUPERVISION AND SUPPORT

'Washing off the grime in pithead time'

This metaphor alludes to the time in mining history when miners were expected to go home filthy from the work and wash at home, carrying the dirt with them into their homes. Eventually this changed and miners were allowed to wash, in pithead time, and not have to do this in their own time.

The analogy with other occupations is that staff should not have to take home the unresolved anxieties and problems from work and try to deal with them in isolation.

It is common in talking and listening to managers to find that they do not get enough support, guidance, praise, training and so on. In essence they do not get enough time and space in which to 'wash off the grime', reflect and get to grips with all the task elements of their jobs. And, of course, this includes you, the reader who is a manager and developer of others. How full is your glass? Empty – you get no support; half empty/half full – you get some support; full – you get lots of support.

In one common situation the senior manager, who should be supervised and supported by the chair of the board, does not receive this input, or receives only part of it. Thus this manager will be giving supervision and support, yet receiving none (or little), which could lead to burnout. The problem must be addressed by the chair and the board of trustees. If it is the case that the chair is not able to offer this, other options should be explored – non-managerial supervision from a paid consultant, mentoring from someone from the same field, or a peer supervision and support group with colleagues from similar organisations.

The support/supervision issue is as relevant to volunteer workers as it is for paid staff, and in some ways perhaps even more so. Volunteers are not there to get paid, but they are seeking some kind of benefit for themselves as well as wanting to help others, so they clearly need input, whether in the form of support or training or of supervision. The remainder of this section looks at the needs of all workers; if you are setting up policies and procedures for volunteers you may need to tailor them to their needs, but overall the same key messages and issues apply.

Staff supervision and support is not an end in itself, but a means to an end. The end is that of ever-improving services that support and empower the client or service user, without adversely affecting the health and well-being of our staff and volunteers. The following diagrams can help put this in perspective:

Supervisor

Practitioner   Service user

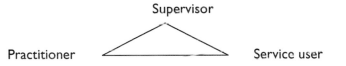

In the first diagram the supervisor has a role to play of ensuring that the needs of the service user are met through the efforts of the worker. The service user should always remain in the picture – the service is there for his or her support.

Managing service delivery

Facilitating
practitioner's
development   Focusing on practitioner's work

In the second diagram the focus is on the worker. His or her work needs to be explored and analysed to ensure its effectiveness, but also the worker has to be considered in order to ensure that he/she is able to grow and develop in the job. Both diagrams are modelled on the work of Hughes and Pengelly.

Exercise: mapping your support and development system

This mapping exercise will clarify the relative positions of people within and outside your organisation. Take a large piece of paper and place an image or symbol of yourself in the middle. Around you, on the paper, draw in (as symbols or letters) all the different sources of support, guidance, development, supervision or inspiration that you experience in and in relation to your work. If there are strong countervailing forces, for example, demotivating factors, include these too.

Different sources could be:

- line manager or committee
- mentor or non-managerial supervisor
- colleagues
- professional or occupational groups
- training courses
- books or programmes.

Place them all in relation to how close/distant or powerful/weak they are. What do you get from each?

Note what different forms the different sources take, for example, formal or informal structures or arrangements.

After you have done this, take another pen and jot down any barriers that get in the way of the sources of support.

What does your map say about the system you work in?

What does your map say about yourself?

Finally, get together with someone and talk it through – someone you trust.

It is fascinating to see revealed the different kinds of systems people work within, and sadly all too common for there to be a clear lack of support and guidance. If this is mirrored in your support and development map, you can take steps to remedy the situation.

This book focuses mostly on the conventional line management supervision arrangement. But some may turn to other sources; mentors can be a valuable source of support, inspiration and experience – people who are experienced in your field and are willing to spend time with you looking at your situation and context. Another option is non-managerial supervision, where you pay an outside supervisor: in this situation, the normal hierarchical relationship does not exist and you can be as open as you like about conditions at work, but you miss out on direct feedback about your performance from someone who knows the setting.

A CORE MODEL FOR STAFF SUPERVISION AND APPRAISAL

An ideal system could be said to be one that integrates ongoing supervision within a longer-term framework of appraisal. Hudson (in *Managing without Profit*) points out that 'supervision needs to be set in the context of individuals' objectives and the support that the organisation has agreed to provide. It flows from the annual appraisal where objectives will have been agreed.'

Schemes should be structured through policies. If organisations work with volunteers appropriate policies can be tailored to meet their support and development needs. An integrated system can empower individuals, groups and organisations as a whole. Morrison (in *Staff Supervision in Social Care*) asserts that supervision can be a major organisational strategy for the protection and empowerment of minority or vulnerable groups – be they staff or clients. In this book supervision and appraisal are viewed as developmental and should therefore be seen as separate from any system of performance-related pay. An integrated system could look like this:

APPRAISAL → SUPERVISION → SUPERVISION → SUPERVISION → APPRAISAL
MEETING   MEETING   MEETING   MEETING   MEETING

Appraisals are usually are at yearly intervals. They take an overview of the jobholder and their year. Intervening supervision sessions can link meaningfully to appraisals. How many supervision sessions occur between appraisals depends on the organisation. Molander and Winterton (in *Managing Human Resources*) argue that 'performance appraisal is fundamental to the entire process of human resource management'.

The functions of supervision

Three major functions of supervision for 'helpers' are identified by Kadushin (as described in *Supervision in the Helping Professions* by Hawkins and Shohet). They are very useful in general managerial terms too.

Managerial
Ensuring agency policies and practices are carried out
Prioritising and allocating work, managing the workload
Setting objectives and evaluating effectiveness, agreeing standards
Clarifying roles and responsibilities
Clarifying role and task boundaries
Maintaining records as per policy.

Learning
Helping staff continue to learn, develop knowledge and skills
Helping team members evaluate their progress

Supporting staff in career development
Understanding workers' value base
Assessing training and development needs
Giving feedback on performance.

Supportive
Enabling people to cope with stress
Developing sensitivity to crises in individuals and teams
Being prepared to step in when people are under stress
Validating person
Safely exploring issues of discrimination
Actively listening/counselling.

Morrison (op. cit.) adds a fourth function:

Mediation
Briefing higher management about resources
Representing staff needs to higher management
Negotiating and clarifying team's remit
Contributing to policy formation
Consulting and briefing staff about organisational developments and information
Advocacy among staff, team and other parts of the system
Dealing sensitively with complaints about staff.

This model suggests that we need to spend a balance of our time as managers of people fulfilling each of the four areas. Interestingly, we know that as people we are more comfortable doing some things rather than others. Some supervisors only ever talk task, task, task with their staff. Others discuss only the more emotional aspects of the work.

Exercise: assessing how you spend your supervisory time

Give examples of what you do in each area, and for how long.

Management
Learning
Support
Mediation

Are you currently not fulfilling any of the functions? If so, why is this? This could be something to discuss with the staff you supervise. What do they think? What do they want?

Staff supervision and anti-discriminatory practice

It is vital to set up structures and processes which include everyone. This way all staff have the same opportunity to learn what is expected of them and to know when they are not meeting the required standards. In some organisations staff from ethnic minorities have suffered discrimination because they have not received the same guidance and feedback as other staff. Supervisors sometimes abdicate from providing the appropriate authority, perhaps because they fear being perceived as discriminatory or because they do not feel the supervisee will respect their authority. Such behaviour might involve not giving staff the necessary feedback they need to correct or improve their performance. In fact, it can lead to the avoidance of supervision on the grounds that 'they' need someone 'special', thus marginalising staff and invalidating their rights.

Practical arrangements for supervision

Supervision cannot work unless certain practical safeguards are in operation:

- dates should be arranged well in advance, for example, two to three months
- all involved need to know how long the session will last.

The length of a session has to relate to how often you meet. If you meet on a one-to-one basis every six weeks then you need at least one hour, or preferably one and a half. If you meet more regularly you may need less time. This also, of course, depends on the needs of the individual.

- sessions should be free of interruptions. They have to be protected
- rescheduling sessions should be the exception, not the rule. Supervision should not be the first thing to be given up.
- this time needs to be in private and not overlooked or overheard in any way
- people need to be comfortable, otherwise they will find it difficult to concentrate for long
- physical barriers – for example, desks between people – should be avoided. Sit at the corners of desks rather than at opposite sides of them, or round a coffee table.

The word 'safeguards' is deliberately chosen. People do not feel safe enough to discuss their concerns frankly unless certain conditions are in place. These safeguards, while not guaranteeing quality discussion, will at least minimise impediments.

Clarity of purpose
Different people mean different things by supervision. However, it normally reflects:

- organisational expectations (you will supervise in this way and at these intervals). This can be generated internally, by management, or externally, by funders

- the supervisor's expectations (different supervisors may give greater emphasis to different functions depending on skill, experience, training and personality)
- expectations of team members, influenced by what people have had before: 'This is the way we do things here' (culture).

Case study: theatre arts organisation

A small theatre arts organisation is headed by a director who manages three project managers. The project managers each manage individual creative projects staffed by artists and volunteers. One of the managers is very unhappy because in her supervision with the director she gets only the managerial element. He seems to be interested only in the task aspects: is this getting done? is that being achieved properly? When she attempts to broaden the agenda the director simply does not listen, but talks over her about the same old things. The project manager is feeling demoralised and unsupported, and wonders if she should leave the organisation.

Luckily, she knows that one of the board members is interested in people management and so she approaches him when he is in the office. They talk, or rather she talks and the board member listens. He then spends some time with the director and is able to suggest diplomatically that the two of them look at what each means by, or wants from, supervision. When they get together, they are able to share perceptions and needs, and to draw up a framework contract for supervision. This specifies that managers need to be able to think out loud, and to be listened to without interruptions and a constant stream of solutions. It also specifies the director's need to be informed about the manager's workload and progress toward deadlines and quality standards.

It is essential to clarify the purpose of supervision and the agreement or contract we intend to work with. Positive understandings do not just happen. They need to be talked about and negotiated. Contracts that just happen are more likely to be flawed or full of holes (i.e. unconscious). This process is just as important for the supervision and support of volunteer workers as it is for paid employees.

It can help to think about supervision in terms of assertive rights and responsibilities:

- supervisors have a responsibility to provide planned, regular supervision
- staff have a responsibility to contribute to their own development
- all have a right to be heard and treated in fair and non-discriminatory ways.

Supervision contracts
Supervision works best when those involved are agreed on the principles of what? why? when? how? who? These include:

- **overall purpose** – a balance of managerial, learning, support and mediation
- **boundaries** – for example, what you will and won't get involved in (personal information); organisational/cultural expectations
- **confidentiality** – who gets told what in which circumstances

- **frequency** – how often? How long?
- **cancellation** – in what circumstances is cancellation acceptable?
- **location** – preferably somewhere quiet and uninterrupted
- **preparation by all parties**
- **content** – to include looking back; looking forward; job description; concerns; information-sharing; planning/setting objectives; any other business
- **recording** – who takes notes? who keeps them? what is the system for paperwork?

Using supervision effectively

In order for supervision to carry out successfully the three (or four) functions both parties need to have an intelligent overview of the role. The aim is to maximise the effectiveness of workers within the agreed or required policies of the agency. To be able to play a meaningful part the supervisor needs to develop a broad picture of what the worker should be doing and of what the worker is doing. This involves reasonable knowledge and understanding of the job purpose and what is required of the jobholder to fulfil it:

- knowledge
- skills or competences
- attitudes and values
- experience.

Supervision will not be effective if the supervisor has insufficient understanding of these. In any job there is a mix of the mandatory (the 'must do') and the desired (what the individual is interested in).

Some useful questions for clarification are:

- do you have a job description?
- is it up-to-date?
- are the objectives for your job clear in terms of what the agency requires?
- what are the results being looked for?
- do you have other objectives for your job?
- have these been discussed?
- have they been agreed?

Structuring a supervision session

A supervision session needs a beginning, a middle and an end.

Beginning Very few people leap straight into the heart of the matter, or the nub of the problem. Why should we? We need time to warm up, relax after rushing around, establish a rapport. Most people will experience some degree of anxiety about having their work focused on, so we need to establish trust.

Middle   The heart of the dialogue, possibly returning to a theme, or a scheduled review of a particular project, the start of a review of a person's role, a continuation of such a review, or explaining what supervision is to someone who is new and inexperienced, or to someone who is experienced in the job but not in being supervised.

The communication skills for this include:

- giving full attention
- asking open questions
- funnelling – moving from open questions to specific probes
- clarifying
- summarising
- reflecting
- listening to what isn't said as well as what is
- giving feedback
- inviting feedback
- reframing or developing new perspectives.

End   Changing the tone: for example, lightening the atmosphere. Timing is important – try to bring things to a close at the appointed time, by recapping on agreements and responsibilities and making the next appointment, if necessary.

Developing an overview

This aspect of supervision draws on some of the general principles of planning and setting objectives. In order to flesh out the overview of any job or role there needs to be a sense of where things are in a continuum. In order to make sense of what is happening now we have to also look back at what happened in the past. Having explored the two together, we can make sensible forecasts for the future.

This needs to take into account what developmental stage the worker is at – is he/she a relative beginner, recently competent or now an accomplished worker who can help others learn?

Look back

What objectives did you set six months ago?
What progress has been made on these?
Which areas of work have been successful for you?
Which areas have been difficult?
Has the necessary or desired support and guidance been available?
Have external factors affected your role?

Look now

What are you working on now?
How does this relate to the objectives of six months ago?
Are there any objectives you need to reaffirm?
Are there any you can drop or transfer?

Are these new objectives?
Do they need discussing with the team?
What are you enjoying?
What are you finding difficult?

Look forward
What are your objectives for the next six months?
What are your needs for resources or training?
What are the priorities for your workload?
Are there any additional responsibilities you want to take on?

These areas are not separate: they run one into another. The aim of the questions is to increase clarity, understanding, insight, to develop the skills of assessment and analysis, to learn what is realistically achievable – for the individual within the framework of the team and the organisation itself.

Setting targets and objectives
Points to consider:

- What is the impact you want to achieve?
- What is the gap between progress made so far and objectives already set (if any)?
- An objective represents the movement from the actual to the desired
- In supervision reflection on, and discussion of, work suggests all sorts of areas where we can usefully set targets. These can surface as difficulties experienced; they can be clarified, new perspectives sought and revised or new objectives set.

A classic acronym is SMART:

SPECIFIC

MEASURABLE

AGREED

REALISTIC

TIME-RELATED.

The above may sound simple, but in practice it may be very hard to keep the focus sharp enough for the process to be followed through. It may also take time – more than one session. Watch out for how you find this when helping another to sharpen up targets. It can help to follow through this process in relation to your own targets.

Giving and receiving feedback

Praise Giving positive feedback motivates people. We feel recognised, valued and encouraged in our efforts. It is a sign that what we are doing does have an impact.

When giving positive feedback, try to:

- genuinely mean it
- be specific
- get the message across clearly i.e. do not mumble
- avoid having a hidden agenda, for example, a favour to ask.

When receiving positive feedback, remember:

- not to make the giver feel silly, by denying it
- respond assertively and genuinely ('Thanks. I was pleased too')
- listen and believe
- there is no need to do it in return
- to show your pleasure.

Criticism   At times the behaviour of others affects the work in such a way that it has to be put right. All of us have blind spots where we are unaware of how we are affecting other people or the situation. Negative feedback then becomes necessary.

When giving negative feedback, try to:

- think it through before doing it
- choose an appropriate time and place
- be clear and specific
- comment on behaviour, not character
- describe rather than judge
- own it ('I felt', 'I thought')
- if appropriate, describe effects of others' behaviour
- do it as soon as possible after recognising the need
- listen to the reply
- think about the outcome you want
- give a positive message as well, if you can.

When receiving negative feedback:

- ask for clarity and examples
- listen
- ask for time to think if you are unsure
- accept what you think is valid
- reject what you don't think is valid
- clarify what is required.

Supervisory style

The style that you have as a supervisor may be crucial in affecting the outcome. But what makes up any one individual's style? It can be easy to assess this in other people, but what about yourself?

Personality   Are you interested in other people, or just in getting the job done? Are you approachable, or off-putting in some way? Can you empathise with others or do you believe personal problems should be left at home? Are you open-minded or do you believe that there is only one way? Are you self-confident or defensive about yourself?

Approaches to control and power   Do you tell, tell, tell? Do you get people involved in joint decision-making or problem-solving? Do you just let people get on with things? Are you open to people of different race or gender?

Experience, skills and training   Have you been prepared for supervising others or were you thrown in at the deep end? Do you have good or bad experiences to look back on? Do you experiment with new skills and approaches? Have you reflected on your level of communication skills?

Exercise: assessing your supervisory skills

Fill in the following questionnaire to assess how you see yourself in relation to the following skills. A '1' is very poor, while a '5' is very skilled indeed. Also, if you are ready to take a risk, ask your line manager or the staff you supervise to fill this in about you.

SELF-ASSESSMENT QUESTIONNAIRE

Knowledge

I understand the purpose of supervision	1	2	3	4	5
I understand the managerial, learning, supportive and mediating functions	1	2	3	4	5
I know the elements of a supervision contract	1	2	3	4	5

Managing sessions

I can explain the purpose and benefits of supervision	1	2	3	4	5
I can negotiate a mutually agreed and clear contract	1	2	3	4	5
I can establish a safe and supportive atmosphere	1	2	3	4	5
I can maintain a balance between the four major functions	1	2	3	4	5
I can end the sessions on time and appropriately	1	2	3	4	5
I can record sessions appropriately	1	2	3	4	5

Intervention skills

I can give feedback in a way that is clear and balanced	1	2	3	4	5
I can focus on both the content and the process	1	2	3	4	5

I can facilitate the expression of feelings	I	2	3	4	5
I can describe my own way of working both in practice and as a supervisor	I	2	3	4	5
I can use open and probing questioning to help others explore	I	2	3	4	5
I can challenge appropriately	I	2	3	4	5
I can develop the skill of reflection in staff	I	2	3	4	5
I can conduct poor-performance meetings properly	I	2	3	4	5
I am sensitive to issues of difference in supervision (ethnic origin, gender etc.)	I	2	3	4	5
I am sensitive to each individual's stage of development	I	2	3	4	5

Personal development

I make sure that my own learning and development takes place	I	2	3	4	5
I recognise my own strengths and weaknesses	I	2	3	4	5
I seek feedback from others: manager, staff, peers	I	2	3	4	5

As a supervisor, or potential supervisor, what are your strengths and weaknesses according to this assessment?

What strengths could you be sharing with others?

What areas are there where you either need to or want to develop?

MANAGING POOR PERFORMANCE

Understanding the causes of an individual's or group's poor performance is crucial. It can be very easy to simply point a finger and assign blame. If you think about situations of poor performance you have witnessed in different settings, you are likely to realise that the causes can be to do with:

the individual
the line manager
the organisation.

As individuals we have unique personalities and needs. This can mean that at times our performance dips (or soars). We may experience events in our personal lives that impact greatly on our work. The same is true of line managers who are responsible for the work of others. Some do not see the need for investing in the performance of others and give no guidance. Some do not have the time. Organisations may not have yet developed the necessary policies and procedures to ensure that managers give both guidance and feedback on individual performance, so that there are no surprises when someone is told that their work is not satisfactory.

Case study: Housing For All (III)

You are the recently appointed co-ordinator of the tenant participation scheme for Housing For All. Relatively new to the post, you are having to drive through various changes as the agency moves into a new phase of organisational development, with new funding and its related requirements. You are involved in steering a new in-house certificated management training programme accredited through the Open College.

One of the related changes you are involved with is that of staff supervision, as you are line-managing three of the staff. Until now there has been no formal structure for this and staff have been able to a large extent to go their own way with the approval or otherwise of the previous very hands-off manager. You are a firm fan of supervision and development, but are also aware that this means quite a culture change. With this in mind you have outlined the purpose and potential benefits of such a system, and also consulted the staff as to their expectations and concerns. So far you have had introductory sessions with each of the staff.

In the last two days there have been two complaints about one of your staff. The first complainant, a new tenant in one of the supported houses, had told another member of staff that he felt he had been treated in a rude and off-hand manner when pursuing what he thought was a reasonable query. The second complainant is a colleague from another agency, an advocacy worker. She has telephoned you to say that the same member of staff has been rude to her. She had made several attempts to obtain some urgent information from your member of staff, but when she finally got to speak to him he had told her that he was not there to run after her. The advocacy worker had challenged him but he refused to discuss it further, saying, 'I don't have time for this.' You have agreed with the advocacy worker that you will discuss this with the staff member and get back to her.

You are not very surprised, as you have noticed one or two occasions when this staff member has responded to others abruptly. Once, for example, you overheard him answering the phone to a member of the public with a curt 'Yes?', without giving his own name or the name of the agency.

Of course, you are very concerned. It is part of this person's job description to work with clients or members of the public in support of their various needs. This is encapsulated in the person specification, which sets out the requirement for interpersonal skills and attitudes and values of respect and consideration for others. On top of this, casework is now clearly governed by stand-ards that stress the necessity of courtesy, respect and speedy attention to people's enquiries.

One of your initiatives has been to set up some customer-care training for the staff and by now most of the staff have done this. Unfortunately, this staff member has not.

When you had your first supervisory session with him the response had been quite negative. He said that they had been working for years without supervision, and that they enjoyed the work and wanted to get on with it without interference. You had explained as well as you could the purpose and benefits, and also told him the bottom line (that it was compulsory, and written into the revised job descriptions).

On the positive side, you are also aware that in various ways you have had a lot of support from this staff member since you arrived. He has been at the agency since it opened, knows the systems and networks inside out and has been willing to guide you. You have a meeting scheduled with this member of staff to discuss the complaint.

As a manager, make an assessment of this scenario. What do you think the causes of this person's poor performance might be? How will you go about handling the meeting to discuss these complaints with him?

How will you open the meeting?
How will you structure the meeting?
What issues and main points will you want to focus on in the discussion?
How will you end the meeting?

Addressing poor performance

If you have a system of staff supervision in place, the battle is half-won already, because if you meet with your staff on a regular basis to set targets and quality standards they know what they have to do and to what standard. As time passes and you review these measures, you will also know how well each person is doing. If you do not take these measures, some day you will face trouble, which will be difficult to deal with because your staff member could say, 'But I didn't realise I had to ...' – and there will be little you can do but start from scratch.

However, even with the best system, carried out well by managers, there will be times when someone needs tackling about something. How will you go about this? Here are some crucial steps and principles to consider.

Preparation: establishing the 'gap'

The gap is that between the responsibilities of the staff member and the standard required for those responsibilities to be fulfilled. If you are clear about this gap, you have something to talk about and which you can explain. In the case study above one of the duties of each staff member is to deal with the public, in accordance with the expected standard of courtesy and respect. If a staff member is rude to a member of the public, this is the gap in question. If, after thinking the situation through on your own (or in your supervision), you decide that you need to tackle this directly, arrange a meeting with the person concerned.

In the meeting: the purpose and the specifics

It is only fair to let people know why you want to talk to them. It may be that if this is an unscheduled meeting, the person will be anxious about it. Explain that you have some concerns to talk about and that you want to hear their perceptions. After this, you need to be specific about what the concern is.

One school of thought recommends that, unless this is in fact a disciplinary meeting, you should start on a general level, giving the staff member a chance to raise the issue him- or herself. An alternative is to begin with positive inputs about the staff member before going on to criticise performance. Another is to come straight to the point: 'I'm afraid I've had some complaints. It seems that ...'

All three approaches are valid, and you have to find what works for you.

Establishing reasons for the gaps

You may not get agreement on there being a gap in the first place. In the above case study the manager has had reports from other people, and has also personally witnessed aprupt behaviour. If you get agreement that there is a gap, you can begin to explore reasons for it. Consider the reasons for poor performance. They could be something to do with any of the following:

- you: the line manager has not set out task requirements clearly, or at all
- the organisation: staff may be operating without job descriptions or contracts, and with little or no supervision, training or development opportunities
- the individual concerned: he/she may just not want to comply with the requirements (misconduct), or may not be able to comply (incapability). Personal reasons may be work-, home- or health-related.

Use the meeting to establish what the reasons are. Use your active listening and feedback skills. Do not start out with a closed mind: you want to bring this person on board so that he/she can give their best for the organisation and its clients. Use the communication and relationship skills outlined in the relevant sections in Chapter 2. Try to apply the principles of assertion: consider rights and responsibilities, and appropriate behaviour in communicating assertively, not aggressively or passively. Avoid personal attack: focus on the behaviour as clearly and precisely as possible. Use your probing skills, as described in the previous section, to go below the surface and find out the substantive reasons for poor performance.

Keep to the point. It may be that the person you are dealing with tends to go off at a tangent. In that case, you will need to use the assertive 'broken record' response: 'I appreciate that you are not satisfied with the pace of change. Can we get on to that once we have cleared up this first matter?'

Another key communication skill to employ is that of summarising – a vital stage in this strained situation. You will have heard a lot of explanation, maybe defensiveness or aggression, and you have to keep track of the main points so they are not lost. By all means jot things down as you go. Summarising is particularly useful when you want to move on to the next stage.

Agreeing the action plan and timescale

If you have agreement about the gap, this will be easier. If not, you need to assert that there is a gap between the level of performance being achieved and the level to which the person must improve. If possible, see if you can obtain the commitment of the person to do what he/she can to put things right, or to do the right thing.

In the case study the scope is there for the manager to feed back some of the very positive things about the person's performance – the fact that he is experienced and has supported the manager in his own induction. This helps. The person you are dealing with may come up with the solution himself; this is the ideal outcome, making commitment to change much easier to secure. If he does not, you need to be prepared with your own suggestions or instructions. Does the staff member need to go on a training course? Is active supervisory guidance on certain aspects of the work required?

Agree what has to be done, how and by when. Arrange a follow-up review to monitor progress and confirm all of this in writing, giving the person a copy to sign.

Follow-up review

This may take place in a normal, scheduled supervision meeting or in a specially organised meeting. If there has been satisfactory progress, confirm this and give positive feedback. Do not forget to stress that the effort must be sustained. Behaviour change is not easy for anyone, and needs reinforcement. Keep offering appropriate support, and follow through. Again, confirm this in writing and give the other person a copy.

If the progress is unsatisfactory, review your options before you meet with the person. Explore the situation as in the first meeting – new factors may have affected the situation. One option is to extend the review period and to set up a new meeting to review again. Another option is to take disciplinary action in accordance with the procedures for the organisation. Do use your own line manager to explore these options before rushing in: managers have suspended staff for gross breaches of the disciplinary code only for the staff member to take out a grievance procedure – and see it succeed.

Incapability and misconduct

Incapability has been defined as inability to perform a role, no matter how much training, exhortation or encouragement is provided, owing to incompetence or ill health.

Misconduct is the failure to exercise skill and care in instances where the employee possesses the necessary abilities but fails to utilise them, thus falling short of the required standards of performance.

In other words, the manager has to discover whether the poor performance is a matter of 'can't' or 'won't'.

DEVELOPING TEAMS THAT WORK TOGETHER AND WELL

Clearly there is an overlap between team development and general group dynamics considerations. A team is one form of group. But it is important to distinguish between teams and groups, as the word 'team' conjures up expectations and assumptions.

A group of community health development workers were quick to focus on this, saying: 'People keep calling us a team – we're not.'

Effective teams

No precise definition of a team exists: much depends on how much time people spend together working toward the same objectives. The community health development workers just mentioned work in different localities, with the same job descriptions, and meet for half a day once a month. They do not constitute a team – but perhaps they constitute a developing community of practice.

Other kinds of group formations could be support and development forums, project or matrix groups and partnership steering groups. Some of the variables that govern teams could well apply to other formations but there will be a difference also.

An effective team (according to the model by Woodcock and Francis) is said to have the following:

- clear, agreed objectives
- climate of support and trust
- open communication
- constructive conflict
- clear procedures
- appropriate leadership
- reviews of progress
- concern for members' development
- good relationships with other groups.

Each of these criteria deserves consideration, to identify what they mean, what can go wrong and some of the possible strategies that can be used to put things right, or get things on the right track.

Clear, agreed objectives
This involves:

- setting objectives and team plans
- clarifying respective team member roles
- agreeing on tolerable differences
- discussing values and reaching consensus on the philosophy of the team
- setting realistic quality standards and reviewing them.

Case study: carers support project (XI)

Over time a split has occurred between those who wanted the group to be based on support and social contact, and those who were also looking beyond this to the possibilities of new technology. Both had been identified as the main objectives for the group, but it was delivering only on one. The project membership needed to revisit these – and to work out how to meet them without alienating existing members.

As long as the needs of members for social support were properly met the group could presumably accept that other people working on the project should address its other aims. Differences between members could surely be tolerated. As part of the review process the group spent time looking again, and afresh, at the project's underlying philosophy.

What can go wrong?	What you can do to put things right
No direction	Clarify your own position through reflection and own line management
Directions from above are unclear or contradictory – or impossible	Clarify your own brief from above – ask assertively for clarity in writing
No agreement in the team on direction – conflict or rebellion	Check what you will insist on and what you will negotiate (your leadership approach)
	Lead appropriate team meetings for going back to basics: planning, team-building, conflict resolution etc.
Individuals refuse to adhere to team policy	Explore with individuals and take action – reinforce norms in the team settings
Role confusion or conflict or overload	Use supervision time individually, and time in meetings if necessary, to clarify
Quality standards are not set	Set standards, in conjunction with over-arching quality systems, in supervision and team meetings

Climate of support and trust
In such a climate:

- relationship-building skills are displayed – conveying respect, genuineness and empathy as core values
- feelings are recognised and managed appropriately
- people's strengths are built on

- people ask for and give support
- people spend time together.

It is important for people to develop effective ways of interacting where regular and significant contact happens between workers.

What can go wrong?	What you can do to put things right
People are rude, put each other down, don't listen	First, check out your own feelings and reactions in supervision
They don't support each other – the focus is all task and no relationship	Explore what others think in their supervision
Personality clashes occur	Can you confront the issue and open up the area for team discussion?
People feel let-down and withdraw (defensiveness)	Is there time in team meetings for people to share some of the process issues – or is it all task?
	Set up new ground rules for team meetings and relationships, model them and challenge others when they don't
	If there are hidden agenda, can they be brought out into the open?

Open communication
If lines of communication are open:

- both positive and critical feedback is given
- each person's contribution to the whole is recognised
- people develop skill at giving and receiving messages in face-to-face communication
- people talk to one another about issues
- people are open to persuasion.

To be able to work like this reflects the forming/storming/norming/performing model of group and team development. The team members have gone through the first uncertain stage of finding out who is who (forming), and of early experiences of testing each other and the group leader out (storming). They have built healthy norms (social rules) of behaviour and communication, and they have worked out who does what, and how they can do things together well (performing).

What can go wrong?	What you can do to put things right
People are told what they do wrong, not what they do right	Praise individuals, privately, and sometimes in the team. Give criticism in private
Managers avoid confrontation through fear	Practise your assertion and confront your own passivity and fears
Staff are not encouraged to develop the necessary 'soft' skills of communication and assertion	Put people on relevant courses, and set up opportunities for talking about how the team is working (process)
People talk behind backs, not face-to-face	Challenge this, set up positive norms and model them
No systems for communication are created	Set systems up. Put aside part of team meetings for asking 'How are we doing?'
An atmosphere of secrets and complaints – the shadow side – exists	Challenge people where you can, bring people in, include everyone. Shine the light on the shadow – open things up for discussion

Constructive conflict

Conflict can be healthy. Constructive conflict means that:

- people deal with issues sooner and in the open where appropriate
- people behave assertively according to a balance of rights and responsibilities
- others are actively encouraged to contribute
- difficulties are seen as normal and dealt with constructively
- unhelpful competition is minimised
- use 'I', not 'you', statements.

This is very similar to open communication in terms of what can go wrong and the strategies for improving things. It is crucial to recognise the importance of the soft skills of communication, and also that they are sometimes very, very hard to put into practice.

Clear procedures

Teams need procedures for:

- structuring and running team meetings
- disseminating information
- making decisions
- written communication between team members
- accessing development and training opportunities.

What can go wrong?	What you can do to put things right
Information not disseminated	Set up a system for sharing information: staff have a right to this as well as a need for it
No written or otherwise clear procedures	If necessary, 'dictate' these; where appropriate, involve the staff in setting them up
Managers chop and change, one minute 'telling', the next 'selling', then simply not caring	Work on your style, to fit both personality, the situation and the maturity of the team
No meetings held	You must have some meetings, their frequency to vary according to the work and need. Hold them for good reasons
Meetings dominated by powerful individuals	Challenge them – privately at first, then in the meetings. Model positive norms and invite quieter people into the process

Leadership appropriate to membership

Appropriate leadership requires that:

- the manager supplies the leadership the team needs
- thus the manager knows the team's strengths, preferences and weaknesses
- the team leader models the philosophy of the team – espoused values are made real
- managers encourage and develop leadership in other team members.

Case study: residential project for young people

This project is a part of a national charity working with children and young people. At a time when the group's residential provision for children is shrinking, this project is under review, which has created great uncertainty concerning staff jobs and futures. The team is also struggling with increased aggression from some of the young clients and some of the key staff have been off on long-term sickness.

The manager decides to hold a team-building event facilitated by an outside consultant who has consulted the staff about what it should cover and how. At one crucial point the team is bemoaning the lack of support and praise they receive. This is discussed and ways of shifting this within the team are suggested. After some time, the manager tells the team that she feels the same and that on some days she feels she is constantly supporting dispirited staff who, on other days, do not even ask her how she is.

This strikes a chord with some in the team, who are able to acknowledge the truth of what she says. They do not think of doing this for her and resolve to look out for her as well as each other.

In this situation the manager is giving a good example of a leadership style that is open and honest, as well as making a clear point. A manager is a person who needs support, as is any member of staff. If one of the team's values is that people will look out for and after each other, this has to include the managers too.

A debate exists concerning the difference between leadership and management. Writers tend to promote leadership as the attractive, egalitarian approach which anyone in the organisation can demonstrate, and which inspires and motivates. In reality, too much is made of the distinction. Of course it is good for all when those who are not managers demonstrate the way forward, but in fact it is part of the manager's job description to take an appropriate leadership approach. Hence, leadership is part of management, whereas management is not necessarily part of leadership.

Remember, the buck stops with you. One of your staff may want to start an exciting new project based on innovative ideas, but you have to decide whether or not the time is right, the money is there, and so on.

What can go wrong?	What you can do to put things right
Inappropriate leadership style adopted by managers (e.g. authoritarian with experienced staff)	Reassess the team, its stage of development and culture (use the road mapping exercise on page 60), then adapt your style to fit the current needs
Talk and action on the part of managers do not match	Be more honest with yourself and others. Do you really prefer to let others get on with things? Then build people up for this
Leadership in others is not actively developed	You must do this. Create or look for opportunities for others to take the lead – in meetings, in representing the project etc.

Reviews of progress
Time is spent:

- reassessing task issues – what the team is doing
- considering the process – how the team is doing it.

Team development is often a matter of concern to managers. Many feel the concept of the team awayday has been overdone, perhaps because it has somehow become associated with over-generous promises or expectations about what it can deliver. Awaydays or team-building events, whether facilitated from within or from without, can be effective if they are held for good reasons and with realistic expectations, can be valuable, but once they have taken place individuals need time to reflect on the discussions and how to use the outputs of the day in future plans.

What can go wrong?	What you can do to put things right
Time is not scheduled in, or not prioritised	Time spent positively can only benefit people – individuals, the team and the clients
The team is defensive about the need for such time	Be gentle. Explain the need and benefits to individuals and the team (start small). Praise developments
Individuals resist change	Explore this in supervision: challenge where necessary, offer training and development, but stress that the bottom line is that this is non-negotiable
A rift exists between manager and team	Explore reasons within yourself, use your own supervision time, heal what breaches you can – if possible, consider an outside facilitator
Time is spent doing reviewing progress, but in a very disorganised manner	Ask others to help in the planning of the time, and become more organised in your own use of time
Time is spent but people get hurt in the process	Create a safe structure, with positive ground rules for behaviour, as well as realism about how deep you can go when trust is lacking
The team gets out of step with the outside world	Use review time to discuss this and to encourage a broadening of the discussion through more contact between this project and others
Objectives and procedures are all imposed	Yes, it is sometimes appropriate to be authoritarian. You may need to insist on a review. Having set this up, you can negotiate certain other matters (content and form).

Concern for individuals' development

The following practices will encourage the personal and career development of individuals:

- regular supervision time allocated to individuals
- opportunities for everyone identified by managers
- team members look out for opportunities for each other
- members look out for their manager
- recognition that people will eventually want to move on to their next challenge.

On the whole, individuals are still very much expected – personally and by others – to be able to cope, whatever the pressure. This is a destructive cultural norm which should be challenged. In a wider context the voluntary sector is expected by government and local authorities to enter into consultation and partnership, but without receiving help with resources – which of course means that voluntary groups and organisations are stretched, if not over-stretched. For an individual, this can mean suffering too much stress, becoming ill, stagnating and becoming cynical – a burnt-out case.

What can go wrong?	What you can do to put things right
No structure exists for staff or volunteer supervision and development	Set one up – there is no excuse for not doing so. Yes, people can sometimes cope without, but they do a lot better with this positive time
Staff see no way forward in their career	Build people up, get them well trained and look for ways forward – or build them yourselves
People do not care for each other	Explore why: are there wounds from the past? Do they need bringing out? Model positive norms, challenge where necessary
The manager is left isolated and unsupported	This happens when the team is worried about itself and forgets that the manager is a human being with needs. Get support from your own line manager or find a mentor – where possible, let the team know you want support too

Good relationships with other groups

Relationships with other groups are positive if:

- the team can co-operate with other projects, agencies or departments
- it actively networks with other parts of the system
- the team actively promotes its services
- it is willing to share its learning and experience with others.

Case study: the drop-in

A well-established project ran a drop-in for people with mental health difficulties. It provided social and emotional support, including various group activities. Many of the clients had been attending the drop-in for years. Some of the staff had been working there for a similar length of time. When a new manager was appointed she was struck by how insular the staff seemed to be in their attitudes to other agencies and their staff. Her staff would tend to dismiss others' efforts and their contribution to the well-being of the drop-in client group. Not only did the staff have this attitude, but they rarely made the effort to visit other agencies and find out what they actually offered.

The new manager was unhappy about this as she believed that the drop-in's own client group was missing out in various ways. Communication breakdowns or gaps were occurring which were blamed on 'them' rather than 'us'. Over time the manager began to address this issue in a variety of ways: in team meetings, which she prioritised; in individual supervision and development; and in directing staff to visit other agencies and to represent the drop-in at various networking forums to do with mental health.

What can go wrong?	What you can do to put things right
Teams can be defensive and build walls rather than bridges	Model your own relationships with others
'Them and us' situation. Projection of fears and anxieties	Invite other staff in to meet yours and discuss similar interests
Managers block using time for the various activities involved	If this is you, change your attitude. If it is your line manager, change his/hers. Persuade, and do it anyway
Individuals lack confidence to make outside contact	Work with people individually to build them up – then raise the expectations from them in this arena. Ask (or rather, tell) them to represent the project at a meeting or to a working party.

4.

Managing quality

This chapter explores:

- the concept of quality
- the difference between self-assessment and external inspection
- quality assurance frameworks as they apply to the voluntary sector
- tailoring your own approach to quality.

What does quality mean to your chief executive? What does it mean to the users of your products or services? What does it mean to your staff? The concept of quality is central to our working lives and must be carefully analysed if we are to understand it and use it positively for the benefit of our organisations, rather than as a stick with which staff are beaten and cowed.

UNDERSTANDING THE CONCEPT OF QUALITY

What does 'quality' mean to you, as a consumer and user of services?

Exercise: consumer power

Think of times when you have been a consumer, paying for services and therefore feeling perhaps some measure of control or power: eating out at a restaurant, or buying something in a shop, for example

What made the experience a good one? If it was a bad experience, why was it bad?

What made the difference between the experiences?

Now think of times when you have been the user of services for which you do not pay, or do not pay directly pay – situations where you might have felt little or no control or power (for example, accessing health care from the NHS, dealing with the benefits service or the state education system).

What experiences of good and poor quality do you recall in these situations? Again, what made the difference between good quality and bad? Did anyone 'go the extra mile' for you?

Your answers to these fundamental questions will shed light on many if not all of the core issues involved in service quality and your managerial and organisational role in it. They will surely touch on matters such as communication, attitudes to customers/service users, time-keeping, efficiency and so on.

Different approaches to quality

The ideas put forward here are based on those of Naomi Pfeffer and Anna Coote of the Institute for Public Policy Research (IPPR) and as such focus on public services in local authorities, education and health services. Their ideas are also relevant to the voluntary and community sectors.

The traditional view

This relates to historical ideas of quality – prestige and superiority. Broadly, this means 'no expense spared', so the final product is perceived as having an aura of quality. Examples might be the Rolls-Royce car and vintage champagne. As such, this interpretation has little relevance to welfare services, though it could be considered in the context of private-sector services.

The scientific or expert approach

This is driven by expert opinion and political power, which prescribes standards of acceptability. It arises out of the machine or scientific management model of organisation and management. It is based on the idea of fitness for purpose: does this service do what it is supposed to? Features and characteristics have to be specified and the specifications become standards that have to be met. The process of quality assurance is a means of enforcing conformance (conformity) to those standards.

There is a strong case for measuring outcomes in any sector. Doing this can help to set benchmarks for good practice and help services develop and staff grow. However, the scientific approach promotes measures of quality which are non-negotiable and set from above. There may be little involvement of users (consumers) in establishing quality measures, and it is very much the case that such schemes were introduced partly to establish control over huge areas of public expenditure and professional practice.

Standards set purely from above can be rigid, frustrating growth and creativity while giving staff mountains of paperwork to demonstrate that the hoops are being jumped through. It is the setting of sets of standards by powerful, usually governmental, bodies which leads to a culture of inspection. Care homes, schools and nurseries and other service establishments are usually monitored and measured against such standards.

The managerial or 'excellence' approach

Within this model, quality is a measure of customer satisfaction, therefore 'getting close to your customers' is the Holy Grail of excellence. Hence the introduction and proliferation of focus groups – ways of bringing together your users, talking to them, and listening to what they want from you.

Many aspects of the excellence approach are radical: for example, the principles of Total Quality Management (TQM). Central to TQM is the principle that everyone is responsible for quality. The roots of this lie in the past. Forty or fifty years ago the Japanese were famous for selling cheap, poor-quality electrical goods. They decided to change the situation, travelled to the West and listened at the feet of Drs Juran and Deming, who were not being listened to in the West.

At that time the Western world was attempting to ensure better quality through increased inspection. This was expensive, meant a high level of rejects and a way of working which was based on compromise. By this time, the Japanese had discovered an alternative – getting things right first time, every time. This prevention-rather-than-cure approach brought about a transformation.

The key principles are:

- everyone is responsible for quality, and everyone is involved, through cross-departmental quality circles, which leads to a culture of continuous improvement
- the concept of the internal customer. Everyone in the organisation is involved in the process chain and is therefore inter-dependent. The secret is to ensure that each link is equally strong – through investing in staff development and finding new ways of working, for example, teamworking on making the whole product instead of isolated individuals performing one process over and over
- the culture of communication in the organisation has to change, with new forums for discussion being introduced, and managers changing their behaviour (learning to listen and ask questions of those who are actually doing the work).

This is an attractive philosophy, but it is not a simple matter to introduce. Most organisations, be they private, public or voluntary, are not predisposed to operate in this way and so cultural issues which could otherwise act as barriers need to be negotiated first. Also, the public and voluntary sectors are not driven by profit and do not have the resources associated with commercial enterprises. The relationship between the user and a service provided by a voluntary organisation is just not the same as that of a consumer paying for a commercial product.

Voluntary organisations often suffer from being resource-starved and having to make hard decisions on this basis. They cannot necessarily meet all the needs of their customers.

When Scope, the cerebral palsy charity, suffered a sharp reduction in income from its shops, it had to refocus its activities and to restructure. It prioritised four areas, which meant that it could no longer help some people as it had in the past. This clearly illustrates the difference between paying and non-paying customers. If the people Scope was able to help in the past had been able to pay directly as commercial customers, Scope could have gone on providing those services. Users of the Scope services may have been delighted by what they received, finding all their expectations fully satisfied, but Scope was going to have to disband that service all the same.

The 'excellence' approach has been associated with the managerialism introduced by the 1979–97 Conservative government, under which, for example, National Health Service managers were given much greater power in order that they could stand up to and overrule professional groupings such as doctors.

The consumerist approach

Here the emphasis is on achieving quality through empowering consumers. The 'excellence' model focuses on providers satisfying customers, while the consumerist approach is about consumers wanting to be satisfied. This puts customers in an active role and increases their power over the decision-making of the providers. Hence, the notion of rights. In a more open market where the customer or consumer has better rights, it is argued, providers will be driven toward quality and the satisfaction of their customers.

Consumer rights include the right to redress, possibly in the form of compensation. Thus, when following a train disaster the rail network was slowed down, customers pursued their right to redress. Compensation could be appropriate if the rail companies can be shown to have failed in their obligations under the contract between themselves and their customers.

Immediate problems arise with this approach in the context of welfare services. For example, if you have poor-quality surgery, you could die; and what could possibly compensate people who have been abused in residential or care homes?

A further problem with the concept of customer power derived from customer choice is that very often there is no choice for recipients of welfare services. Services are under-resourced, so if you need the services of a chiropodist, for example, there may be no alternative hospital to go to and you may not be able to have your feet seen to as often as you need. A further problem is that when organisations are failing to meet what people's rights lead them to expect they can be punished: 'named and shamed'. But this will not improve morale or strengthen staff loyalty. How do you balance the rights of staff to feel good about what they do against the rights of the customer/user of a service?

Making the public more powerful

Having assessed each of the above four approaches to quality and their impact in welfare settings, Coote and Pfeffer proposed a new model which drew on each of the scientific, excellence and consumerist approaches.

An open system	Mostly	To some extent	Not much
Our users know what services we provide and how to apply			
They know the bases on which decisions are made about them			
They have information to help them take part in decision-making			
They know how to complain and appeal			
They know how our services are planned			
They have information about the outcomes of our work			
They know the criteria for any targeting or rationing			
They know how to affect decision-making			

Public participation

A democratic approach to the pursuit of quality will depend on the public taking an active part in decisions about what constitutes a quality service. If there is money in an area to improve health, the professionals might believe that what is needed is another midwife, but if you ask the community they might say they need better parks and play areas.

Involving the public in a quality initiative will depend on the availability of the following:

- a strong infrastructure to support different forms of public participation
- the relevant information
- clear rights so that people can take part in different stages of decision-making
- proper support for representatives and channels through which they can communicate with those they are representing
- enough space and resources for public meetings
- ways to ensure the views of those who cannot take part are taken into account
- collecting and publicising information about decisions taken and how they affect the public.

Choice and building a responsive system

Within this model is scope for widening collective choice through service agreements and opening up decision-making. Individual choice can be widened too. The experts are not always right and there can be room for negotiation. In my own experience in mental health care I remember making people go into activity groups because it was 'good for them' rather than acknowledging that this was about staff control and power. Within a system where the primary goal is to give everyone an equal chance, but resources are limited, it is still possible to spread information properly and then to negotiate with the public about how these resources are allocated.

Involving the workers and changing management and professional cultures

Staff morale and motivation are crucial to the effective delivery of a quality service. People working as staff in voluntary organisations are doing so on the whole because they want to do something worthwhile that makes a difference to others. They also need to be fully involved in service-planning and decision-making. As far as management and professional cultures go it is essential to provide flexibility, transparency and an inclusive approach to planning and decision-making.

Ensuring fitness for purpose

Finally, within this democratic model of quality, systematic auditing is essential. It should be based on specifications agreed with users, not imposed on them, and using methods of review which take into account users' needs and experiences. How well does your organisation do against the principles of this model?

Case study: Housing For All (IV)

This organisation has been in difficulties (see page 93). The director had responded to the new situation by doing more of what he had already done, which, unsurprisingly, has not worked, and the management committee has finally become involved – in a constructive manner. We considered what analysis to make and what changes to recommend. The director just could not change his (authoritarian and controlling) style and in the end agreed to resign, following pressure from a key faction on the management committee.

A new director has been appointed, after consultation led by the chair of the committee with the staff as a group, and she is now in post. Her brief is to create a whole new culture and for this to be mirrored in any structural changes made. The culture is to revolve around a positive view of staff involvement and the values of participation and respect.

The new director has taken this on board, immediately setting up a forum to discuss how to move the organisation forward. This meets monthly for two hours. At the second meeting of the forum the director explained that a major funder had become aware of their recent internal difficulties and was now insisting that Housing For All sign up to a recognised quality assurance framework. The funder had suggested that it would prefer the EFQM Excellence Model (formerly the Business Excellence Model), because this was being promoted by the NCVO Quality Task Standards Group, but would consider another recognised scheme if argued for.

The director admitted that her heart had sunk when this was put to her, but that since then she had decided to see the demand as an opportunity to progress the organisation in the way that they already knew they wanted to. She proposed setting up a quality working group to explore the different models and to recommend to the management committee which to choose and use.

Exercise: quality assurance

Consider the following quality assurance schemes in relation to both your own organisation and to Housing For All. Which scheme would help take the organisation forward?

SELF-ASSESSMENT AND EXTERNAL INSPECTION: HOW THEY DIFFER

Inspection

Many organisations, especially in the public sector, are now required to have external inspection – for example, Ofsted inspects schools. As a form of quality control, the inspections have been much debated over the years.

Under some systems of external inspection organisations invite (and pay) another body to assess them on various criteria and standards. These organisations can be awarded some kind of quality kitemark: for example, Investors in People or the Charter Mark. The main systems will be considered below as they apply to the voluntary sector. These are voluntary forms of inspection, offering the chance to see the organisation's performance through the eyes of independent assessors who have knowledge of other similar enterprises and can therefore also offer benchmarking opportunities. But a weakness of these systems is that they may be expensive for smaller or medium-sized organisations.

Self-assessment

Organisations can adopt a framework which they apply to themselves, examining their practices and procedures with a view to improving them. Self-assessment has the merit of being self-driven and flexible, allowing off-the-peg systems to be altered to suit, and presumably being triggered by organisations wanting to demonstrate better practice on behalf of their clients. This approach to quality is also more likely to promote ownership of the improvement process.

Quality frameworks are often linked to the requirements of external agencies. Funders within the contract culture may well require certain specifications or outcomes to be set, and reviewed regularly. Even if an organisation is not required by an external body to use a quality framework, it still makes a great deal of sense for it to find or generate some framework that suits it and its users.

Exercise: quality quiz

Become familiar with the building blocks of quality assurance. How many of the following do you understand? For each one write a brief definition.

Minimum standards
Benchmarking
Stakeholders
Continuous improvement
Quality circles
Added value
Input-output-outcome
Performance indicator
Right first time
Focus groups
Self-assessment
Fitness for purpose
Mission statement
Internal customer

And the answers are:

Minimum standards	Standards below which a service must not fall
Benchmarking	Comparing your practice with that of excellent organisations in the same or different fields
Stakeholders	Groups of people with a significant interest in a service or organisation
Continuous improvement	Philosophy of always looking for better ways – for everyone – and implementing them
Quality circles	Staff from different levels and departments getting together to improve processes and outcomes
Added value	Improving the lot of a person or service by means of a specific process
Input-output-outcome	Input = what goes into processes, for example, staff, buildings, money. Output = what the processes create, for example, advice sessions, supported housing. Outcomes = what difference is made by this, for example, empowered people complaining, people living independently
Performance indicator	Concrete example that demonstrates the meeting of a standard, for example, allowing patients their own clothes is an indicator of giving people respect and choice
Right first time	Approach to quality that urges prevention of problems/defects rather than cure

Focus groups	Groups of users or customers who are brought together to discuss services and products in order for deliverers to improve them
Self-assessment	Voluntarily adopted system to improve, using internal assessment of progress
Fitness for purpose	Ability to carry out function for which created
Mission statement	What the organisation seeks to achieve and what impact it wants to make – in a nutshell
Internal customer	Anyone inside the organisation who works interdependently with others, and is responsible for the quality of what they pass on

QUALITY ASSURANCE FRAMEWORKS AND THE VOLUNTARY SECTOR

A number of quality assurance schemes apply to the voluntary sector:

- Quality First – a self-assessment framework for very small groups or projects
- *Self-assessment Workbook: Measuring Success*
- PQASSO (Practical Quality Assurance System for Small Organisations) – self-assessment
- EFQM Excellence Model (now usually referred to simply as the Excellence Model) – self-assessment and award
- Social Audit – voluntary inspection (usually by an external person)
- Investors in People – voluntary inspection
- National Standards and Best Value – compulsory inspection
- Quality Mark – compulsory inspection for some groups.

Each of these is outlined below, and recommendations for further reading are given at the back of this book.

Quality First

This system for very small projects with no paid staff was developed by Birmingham Voluntary Services Council (BVSC) and Tony Farley. Quality First is based on four principles:

- say what you do
- do what you say
- monitor and review progress regularly
- see improvement as a result.

The framework covers nine areas of work:

- stating the purpose
- standards and values
- managing it all
- involving the community
- working together as volunteers
- equality and fairness
- reviewing our work
- financial management
- communicating effectively.

It is designed as a continuing process, not a standard of attainment. A workbook (price £25 or free to groups in Birmingham: see Further Reading and Resources) is available. The method is to compile a portfolio of evidence to show that the project is working to either Level 1 or Level 2 in terms of progress in each area, and for each area a statement acts as a standard. For example, for 'Involving Our Community' the statement is: 'We will make sure that people who use our services are satisfied and that they are encouraged to contribute to the running of the organisation and to reviews of our work.'

Case study: Save Our Park!

A group of people got together to see what they could do about their local park and play area. Over the years it had become run-down, and the play area had been vandalised and was being frequented by drug users. Save Our Park!, as the group called itself, had been meeting as a group in the community and was beginning to meet with council representatives to discuss the future of the park. One of the group was interested in looking for funding to help with the project.

A project development worker from the local Council for Voluntary Service heard about the group and met with them. She recommended that they use a quality framework, such as Quality First, designed for very small project groups, to help them develop their skills and capacity as a group. This would strengthen their case for funders to take them seriously. The group agreed to give it a try.

Self-assessment Workbook: Measuring Success

This scheme, developed by the Quality Standards Task Group at NCVO, is based on a workbook which costs £5 to buy but can also be downloaded free from the internet (see Further Reading and Resources). The structure is simple and effective. It is in four main parts:

Part 1: Self-assessment
This is divided into seven sections that cover most of what an organisation does. When completing the self-assessment you are asked to answer three statements in each section, which form the relevant standards. You then list strengths and areas for improvement

Part 2: Prioritising areas for improvement

Part 3: SMART goals
This helps you turn priorities into manageable goals

Part 4: Keeping track of SMART goals (see page 89)
The seven sections covered are:

- the whole picture
- customers
- leadership
- making plans
- people
- partnerships and resources
- ways of working.

Practical Quality Assurance System for Small Organisations (PQASSO)

This scheme was developed by Charities Evaluation Services and Tony Farley specifically for use by small voluntary organisations and by smaller project groups within larger organisations. It has 12 standards, each at three levels, covering all aspects of an organisation's work. Each standard carries performance indicators to demonstrate the meeting of that standard. You can assess your own organisation or project for each standard by assessing whether it is: not met, just started, making good progress or fully met.

The 12 areas are as follows:

- planning for quality
- governance
- management
- user-centred service
- staff and volunteers
- training and development
- managing money
- managing resources
- managing activities
- networking and partnership
- monitoring and evaluation
- results.

The scheme is user-friendly.

Governance: meeting your responsibilities

The standard: The organisation ensures that it governs itself effectively and responsibly. It demonstrates accountability to the appropriate bodies and people, and the board of trustees has the skills and information it needs to achieve its mission.

Level 1

The board meets all its legal duties, provides basic management support and is accountable to funders and other stakeholders.

Indicators and suggested evidence

Trustees receive an induction into the organisation and understand the mission and aims.
Evidence: trustee induction pack containing the organisation's mission, aims and other important information
Trustees understand their overall responsibility for the organisation and declare any conflict of interest.
Evidence: documents about trustee responsibilities, for example, policies on employment, health and safety, finance, insurance and conflict of interest
Trustees work within the constitution and ensure that all other legal requirements as a charity and/or as a company are met
Evidence: constitution and annual report
Arrangements are made to get necessary work done.
Accurate minutes are produced of decisions and of actions agreed.
Evidence: minutes of meetings and plans for delegated actions
All trustees attend most meetings, and oversee organisational policies and practices
Evidence: records of attendance at meetings, and minutes that deal with organisational policies
Trustees ensure that a budget is agreed, and that they receive financial reports as planned and that financial and auditing requirements are met
Evidence: budgets, financial reports and audit reports

Level 2

The board actively takes responsibility for strategic planning and ensuring effective management, and it evaluates the work of the organisation

Indicators and suggested evidence

Trustees have a planned, annual programme of meetings, including time to discuss specific issues in depth
Evidence: schedule of board meetings and sub-group meetings
The roles and responsibilities of the chair, secretary and treasurer are clear
Evidence: documented roles and responsibilities
Trustees have opportunities for training and development
Evidence: training records

Trustees contribute fully to the strategic plan, and agree other more detailed plans
Evidence: board papers and minutes of meetings, strategic and other plans
Trustees support the senior managers and hold managers accountable for the working of the organisation and the results achieved
Evidence: records of support meetings and progress reports
Trustees receive regular information that shows them what the organisation is achieving
Evidence: progress and funding reports

Level 3

The board works in a professional way with managers and staff to achieve excellent results and a high-quality organisation

Indicators and suggested evidence
Trustees work well as a team, and review their own effectiveness regularly
Evidence: minutes of review meetings and awaydays, records of training sessions
The board reviews its membership for the skills and knowledge it needs and recruits people according to those needs
Evidence: results of reviews and skills audits
Trustees add value to the organisation by reflecting the diversity of the local community
Evidence: profile of the board of trustees
Arrangements are made to appraise the director every year
Evidence: records of appraisals
Arrangements are made to appraise the director every year
Evidence: records of appraisals
Using the results of monitoring and evaluation, the trustees show that the organisation's activities are cost-effective
Evidence: evaluation results and unit cost reviews

(from *PQASSO: quality standard for governance*)

Exercise: assessing your organisation

Assess your own organisational level. Where would you say your organisation sits? Carrying out such an assessment of any of the areas can offer plenty of scope for organisational development, for discussion with users and staff, and will provide action points as and when you see the gaps. You may not be able to carry out a review of all 12 areas at once: do one at a time, allocate responsibility to specific staff members, or to mixed groups of staff and users.

The strengths of a scheme such as PQASSO are that it is relatively simple, can be carried out over time and is truly developmental. The documentation is also inexpensive, retailing at approximately £50 (and also available on CD-ROM). It is more detailed than the *Self-assessment Workbook* in that it sets out what the standards are at three levels – a strength, in that the thinking is done for you. However, you may take the view that it is worth doing the thinking for yourself, depending on a your organisation's philosophy and its resources.

EFQM Excellence Model ('Excellence Model')

This important model for the voluntary sector has been recommended by the Quality Standards Task Group (QSTG) at NCVO, which has also recommended that the voluntary sector should:

- adopt and work to a set of quality principles
- commit to the concept and practice of continuous improvement
- introduce and develop the Excellence Model.

(from *Quality Standards in the Voluntary Sector*, briefing paper, March 1988)

We can recognise some of the concepts as belonging to the excellence approach to quality as outlined by Coote and Pfeffer above. This is the language of TQM (Total Quality Management). Unlike the PQASSO model, this has its roots in the private sector, although it is increasingly being used in the public sector. Charities Evaluation Services offers courses on the business model as well as on its own PQASSO approach. The QSTG has produced a guide to the Excellence Model for voluntary organisations called *Excellence in View*.

Firstly this Excellence model separates *'enablers'* from *'results'*: all are termed *criteria*.

⇐ ⇐ ⇐ Enablers ⇒ ⇒ ⇒ ⇒ ⇒   ⇐ ⇐ ⇐ Results ⇒ ⇒ ⇒

Leadership	People		Processes	People	Key performance results
Leadership	Policy and strategy		Processes	Customer	Key performance results
Leadership			Processes	Society	
	Partnerships and resources				

⇐ ⇐
Learning and innovation

In brief, the above criteria translate as:

Enablers

- leadership: how leaders set the direction of the organisation and encourage people to achieve the right results
- policy and strategy: how the organisation sets out what it wants to achieve and the way it will do it
- people (staff): ensuring that staff and volunteers know what is needed, have the skills, and are motivated, supported and rewarded
- partnerships and resources: enabling ways of working in partnership and resource management that work
- processes: designing and managing ways of working so that services are delivered efficiently, effectively and to the standard required to meet customers' needs and expectations.

Results

- customer results: what the organisation is achieving for its external customers, the users or clients, or key stakeholders
- people results: what the organisation is achieving for its staff and volunteers – what they are getting out of the equation
- society results: obviously a key determinant for voluntary organisations as social organisations, these reflect the relationship between organisation and wider society
- key performance results: how well the organisation has achieved what it set out to.

Enablers		⇒ ⇐	Results	
	People 9%		People 9%	
Leadership 10%	Policy and strategy 8%	Processes 14%	Customer 20%	Key performance 15%
	Partnership and resources 9%		Society 6%	

Although this method is largely one of self-assessment, it is possible to apply for a regional or national award based on use of the framework over time, which would include inspection and feedback.

The Excellence approach to self-assessment: a taster

Score the following according to how well they are met. A = fully met, B = partly met, C = not done/don't know

Customer results
(1) We regularly collect and review information on how the organisation is perceived by, and performs for, all its customers
(2) Customer satisfaction targets have been set and all staff are committed to meeting them
(3) Information from customers is used consistently to improve the way the organisation works

Key performance results
(1) Our organisation knows what key results it wants
(2) We systematically collect evidence on how well we are achieving those results
(3) The evidence we collect is used systematically to produce improvements

People results
(1) Our well documented evidence shows that our organisation has a culture of satisfied and motivated staff
(2) Staff give regular feedback which is used systematically to produce improvements
(3) Internal communication is monitored and we set targets for improvements

Society results
(1) Strong evidence shows that our organisation is a 'good citizen' in the communities in which it is based
(2) Information on our organisation's reputation and profile in the community is collected and reviewed. We have positive trends
(3) Our organisation works with partners to produce improvements for society

Leadership
(1) Managers/leaders actively develop mission and values
(2) We use feedback to change the way that the organisation is managed
(3) Managers/leaders are actively involved with staff and customers in creating improvements

Policy and strategy
(1) When plans are produced they take into account everyone who has a direct interest in the organisation
(2) Our plans and strategy are continuously reviewed to assess what they are achieving
(3) Our plans and strategy are based on a broad range of internal and external information about our performance

People

(1) Creativity and innovation are encouraged at every level
(2) The performance of all staff is effectively appraised and positive feedback provided
(3) All staff are supported in their personal aspirations and career development

Partnerships and resources

(1) All our resources are deployed to maximum effect in achieving our aims and objectives
(2) We work well with external partners to support and develop what the organisation does
(3) Technology is used efficiently and effectively

Processes

(1) Our key processes are understood, well-managed and continuously improved
(2) Information on our organisation's performance is used to review and improve its ways of working
(3) Our ways of working and procedures are designed and developed around the needs and expectations of our customers

(from *Excellence in View*)

The Excellence Model promotes the path of dialogue and consensus. You can use the above as a taster with your team or committee to see how well you believe your organisation is doing. The approach as a whole carries with it a full set of questions, standards and performance indicators which organisations can facilitate themselves or through peer review with other organisations (one networking group that exists for this purpose can be accessed via the QSTG/British Quality Foundation) or hire a consultant to manage.

Scoring and weighting is a further option, but most voluntary and public sector organisations choose not to do so, and it is generally accepted that scoring is a distraction in the first few years. It becomes significant only when organisations start to think about awards.

Some examples of ways of implementing the model are:

• teams work through the model analysing a current situation and using the questions in the *Excellence in View* guide
• using a questionnaire based on the model
• using workshops to gather evidence from individuals across the organisation on how the nine criteria are being met. Most start with the results criteria and then collectively assess the evidence according to strengths and areas for improvement
• an award simulation whereby the organisation produces a detailed document describing what it is achieving under each criterion and sub-criterion. A team of assessors tests the report and identifies strengths and areas for improvement. A score is agreed for the organisation and the management team develops and monitors an action plan based on the assessment
• using one of a variety of software packages for conducting and analysing an Excellence self-assessment.

A strength of the Excellence approach is that it is more detailed and sophisticated than the first two models described in this section. The weightings put a 'price' on how important each criterion is; hence, if you accept these prices this could be a very useful framework to adopt. However, as Excellence is a more complex scheme it will take more time to understand and implement it, which may make it less attractive to smaller organisations.

It is possible to start using the Excellence model without incurring any cost other than time. However, if training on the model is required, Charities Evaluation Services can provide it. The guide to the model, *Excellence in View*, can be bought from NCVO (See Further Reading and Resources).

If at a later stage you wish to apply for a regional or national award, a fee will be payable, but most regional Excellence centres offer discounts to voluntary organisations. The Quality Standards Task Group at NCVO publishes information (including case studies) on the use of the Excellence Model in the voluntary sector on the NCVO website (see Further Reading and Resources).

Social Audit

This approach is radically different from those outlined above. While those already described are essentially off-the-peg systems with closely defined structure and content, Social Auditing places emphasis on developing a collective approach with the organisation's main stakeholders. Having been identified, these people or organisations are consulted in order that key issues can be defined and performance indicators devised. Social Auditing is therefore a judgement by those directly affected by an organisation, based on criteria they have themselves specified. As in the Excellence and Investors in People models the organisation does the work itself. It can then choose to be audited independently.

This approach, orginally designed to test private companies' accountability to the people and communities they affect, is now being adopted by voluntary organisations that want to root their activities firmly in the needs and opinions of their stakeholders. Proponents of Social Auditing with voluntary organisations are recommending that the Quality Standards Task Group at NCVO should examine this approach as a means of ensuring accountability and as a tool for developing transparency and evaluation.

Investors in People

The Investors in People Standard was launch in 1990 after research into what makes an organisation successful. It was formed through a partnership between government, employers and employee representative organisations, businesses, the Confederation of British Industry, the Trades Union Congress, the Chartered Institute of Personnel and Development and the National Training Task Force.

The Standard can now be delivered to all UK employing organisations regardless of size or sector through systems operating through local Learning & Skills Councils or Business Links and their counterparts in Scotland, Wales and Northern Ireland. If you approach the Investors in People team at your local LSC or Business Link delivery organisation it will explain the Standard and the process at an initial meeting, and, if you wish, carry out a diagnostic exercise to see where your organisation sits in relation to the Standards. This will lead to an action plan and assessment. The delivery organisation will advise you on charges and any available subsidies. The final assessment costs up to £550 per day and for a 50-person organisation this might take two to three days.

Investors in People is not only for the bigger organisations: Age Concern in Leeds, which has 21 staff (supported by 150 volunteers), has achieved Investors in People status. Its chief officer is very positive about the process, and has said: 'The main benefits for the organisation are that we have clear policies that are written down in one place and our training is more focused and better managed.'

The Standard is based upon four principles: commitment, planning, action and evaluation. Each of these has supporting indicators and evidence requirements.

The Standard concentrates upon the organisation's core assets – its people – and is based on the human resources principle that if you involve and develop your people in the right way this will continually strengthen the effectiveness and outputs of the organisation. In the private sector, Investors in People is said to have the potential to increase the productivity and profitability of the enterprises and can be used as a business improvement tool to support other initiatives.

National Standards and 'Best Value'

The 'Best Value' system is a cyclical mechanism, the purpose of which is to drive local authorities to make continual improvements to their services. Councils are required to draw up annual Best Value Performance Plans (BVPPs), which are designed to allow discussion with the community about spending priorities. The Audit Commission, along with the government, has specified performance indicators for key council services that are intended to serve as a yardstick for assessing local performance.

The Best Value Performance Plan should include:

- a summary of the council's objectives
- a summary of current performance and a comparison with the previous performance
- a summary of the council's approach to achieving improvements in efficiency
- a plan and timetable for Best Value reviews and a summary of the results of completed Best Value reviews
- performance targets for future years along with action plans for achieving them
- a statement setting out how the council will consult with the community
- a response to audit and inspection
- a financial statement.

Central to Best Value are the 'four Cs':

- challenge: should this service be provided at all and, if so, is it being provided in the most effective way?
- consult: the local authority must find out what the local population wants and is prepared to pay for
- compare: benchmarking – in order to develop better organisational practice
- compete: who can best deliver this service to the desired quality at the lowest cost?

A report on the local authority's Best Value Performance Plan is made by the external auditor by 30 June each year, and since April 2000 all council activities have been inspected. The Audit Commission is responsible for inspecting all services not inspected by other bodies: for example, OFSTED and education, the Social Services Inspectorate and social services, the National Care Standards Body and residential care services.

How does Best Value affect voluntary organisations? It will affect any organisation that has a relationship with a local authority – grant-aided groups, those working to a contract and those working in a partnership. Over a five-year period councils are required to subject all their activities to a review. This process is not laid down in detail for local authorities as each may interpret the four Cs in its own way, but it is the four Cs which will inform the review process.

Any voluntary organisation already engaged in one of the above-mentioned major quality assurance schemes will already be preparing itself well for any review process under Best Value.

Choosing a quality framework

Case study: Housing For All (V)

Having considered the different frameworks for quality, talked to staff from organisations using each of them and attempted to match its situation with one system, the quality work group ended by recommending the use of PQASSO. At first the group had been very enthusiastic about Investors in People as it was so positive about staff and staff development, and given the recent experience of being starved of such input the group had nearly opted for this approach.

It was at this point that the director had expressed reservations: surely they needed a scheme which was wider in its scope than IiP appeared to be? They needed an approach that was all-inclusive and would offer every aspect of the organisation a chance to grow and develop.

Others slowly agreed and the options under discussion thereafter were PQASSO, Excellence and Social Audit. Some of the team were initially keen on Social Audit because it would give their stakeholders a prominent part to play. But after a while the majority view emerged that HFA needed a system that allowed the organisation to heal itself from within. The team also felt that it needed a system based on self-assessment, within a structure that was inclusive but not too complex. For some, this ruled out Excellence, as the percentage ratings accorded to the different criteria seemed to be out of line with Housing For All's priorities, and the model was felt to be potentially too prescriptive in terms of its key components.

To the group it appeared that PQASSO had what the organisation needed – a structured framework that could adapt to HFA's situation and size. Most importantly, the group believed that this was a model that all staff would be able to understand and to take part in. The organisation needed everyone to be involved in order to continue the healing process and the transition to a new era and culture of work. They felt that they would be in a position to move on to use of the Excellence Model over time.

PQASSO was recommended to the management committee and accepted.

Exercise: the right scheme

What scheme did you think would be right for Housing For All, and why? Remember, there could be more than one right answer.

A useful checklist covering actions to take when setting out on the journey of quality development is given in the Quality Standards Task Group newsletter:

- recognise that implementing quality principles usually means a change in organisational culture. This must begin from the top – with the board and senior management – and be communicated throughout the organisation
- take it one step at a time
- review what you already have done, and build on this
- appoint an individual or group to co-ordinate the process
- locate the quality process within your strategic planning
- get the views of all your key stakeholders – staff, users, referrers, funders etc.
- base your standards/service promises on the above consultation and your own core values
- evaluate the different schemes for quality and ask for advice from your local CVS or NCVO.

TAILORING YOUR OWN APPROACH TO QUALITY

This section is for you to begin to think about yourself as a manager or responsible person considering how you can focus your efforts on better outcomes.

Radical incrementalism – the 'one per centers'

Every long march starts with a single step – but the good news is that if you take one step every day you will at some point realise that you are really travelling. Just don't try to do it all at once. Do one small thing each day. If the filing system is in a mess but you cannot set aside two to three hours as suggested in the time management exercise in Chapter 2, simply give it 10 minutes every day (without fail) and the filing system will in due course be sorted out. Remember, one per cent every day for 50 days adds up to 50 per cent, and once a point of critical mass is achieved, the energy invested will have a real impact.

Exercise: 'one per centers'

What three 'one per centers' can you identify right now?

Creative swiping

This is benchmarking by another name. We all see good ideas as we travel about and carry out our work – so borrow or copy them and make them work for your organisation and people. Think about this – what great ideas for work practices or methods have you come across recently? How can you use them in your own work?

Paradigms

A paradigm is a way of viewing the world – 'thinking inside the box' and not being allowed to look outside it. For example, the Christian Church ruled that the sun rotated around the earth and anyone who said otherwise faced execution. A more recent example might be the assumption that those who are professionally qualified and trained know best what should happen in a situation regarding service users. This may not be the case. Paradigms can give us a false sense of security and the feeling that the times are a-changing is a scary one.

'Sacred cows'

All organisations, large or small, have sacred cows. At times the sacred cow will block the road to new ideas and progress. What are they in your setting? Could it be that because the rota has always been done in a certain way it can never be done in a different way? Does the assumption that 'we could never afford that kind of technology!' mean that you should not work your socks off to get it, because it will transform the way you work?

Exposing the sacred cows is the task of the process observer – if you are not a process observer you may not be aware of any sacred cows. Letting go of the old ways is hard – it involves loss – and loss is difficult for most people, even if the initial loss will lead to overall gain.

Exploring new ways

Are there any new and exciting ideas you could turn into the next generation of sacred cows? (Whatever is the latest good idea will in time become just another sacred cow.) Could your project be the best for delighting your end users? Could you go for having the most up-to-date and effective technology you can find?

Oddbods

Make a list of all the 'oddbods' in the organisation and listen to them. All too often we are afraid of those who rock the boat, but maybe it is now time to cherish them. Listening is the key here, and surely listening is at the heart of quality assurance. What is it that people need? What is it that people want? How do they want us to deliver it? If people are critical, we need to listen to them, and if possible to learn. If they say, 'Why can't we …?' can you explore the question, preferably by discussing it with the questioner?

Research on the sources of invention recognised that many major inventions, ranging from the ballpoint pen to penicillin, happened in the 'wrong' place. They were invented by individuals not in a company, or by a very small company, or by an individual in an 'out group' in a large company – or by a large company in the 'wrong' industry. In other words, these inventions were made by some kind of 'oddbod'.

Aside from the 'oddbods', keep asking people, 'How did we do?' 'Did we do what we said we would do?'

Businesses pay 'mystery shoppers' to test out what kind of service is available in different kinds of situations. How can you test the interface between your staff and your clients, in an ethical but effective way?

Get personal about quality

You may have discovered that when someone goes the extra mile for you it can have a profound impact.

Recently, when booking flights to America to visit my children, I realised, belatedly, that I had booked the wrong return date. I had booked to come home a day early, so I would needlessly miss out on a whole 24 hours with them – time that we needed. Although I had signed documents which said that changes were not permitted and that cancellation would cost a lot of money, I contacted the travel agent to explain, and to ask for help.

The travel agent went to great lengths to explain the situation to the airline, and succeeded in getting me the very last seat on a plane coming back the next day. I was immensely relieved, and I am certain I will go back to that travel agent.

Go the extra mile for your clients, go the extra mile for your staff, and the transformation will be tangible.

5.

Marketing

If management is about doing the right things well, then marketing is about working out what the right things to do are in the first place: finding out what your customers want (and/or need) and delivering it to them profitably.

Voluntary organisations may be "non profit" in the commercial sense, but that doesn't mean that you don't need to make money. Building sustainable streams of earned income is key for many voluntary organisations as traditional sources of income dry up in order to ensure their long-term independence and sustainability.

By applying marketing techniques you can make sure that you are offering services that your customers want and know how to access.

In essence, the fact that your organisation was set up is a prime example of good marketing – identifying and fulfilling an unmet need.

NOT JUST SALES

Too often marketing is seen as just being "sales" (and often, implicitly, selling things that people don't want or need). At best a necessary evil, at worst, an activity at odds with your core purpose.

But what is marketing?

Put simply, marketing has been defined as getting the right product in the right place at the right price, and promoting it so everyone knows about it.

Too often, organisations fall into the trap of seeing marketing as a remedy, as something to be called in as an emergency measure to boost flagging income levels or to produce a leaflet to raise awareness. But successful organisations know that marketing needs to be at the heart of all business activities, influencing everything from service development to delivery.

This chapter looks at some core areas of marketing, including segmentation, competitive positioning, branding and the marketing mix, and at how they can be integrated into the management function.

SEGMENTATION, TARGETING AND POSITIONING

The voluntary sector market place is very large. There are now some 140,000 registered charities in the UK and many more voluntary organisations. With this amount of competition (for funders and/or supporters), effective marketing becomes even more important.

Segmentation

Segmentation, as it sounds, is the process of dividing up your market into groups with shared attributes to enable you to enable you to develop and target your products and services more effectively. There are many criteria for segmenting markets, for example in terms of size, buying behaviour, location or cause.

However, from a marketing perspective the most effective criterion is simply to segment on the basis of benefits sought. This may of course incorporate some or all of the criteria above (for example, it is reasonable to assume that organisations in the North West of England would be like events to be held in that region) but looks at the segmentation process from the customer's perspective – what do *they* want from you?

Remember that a benefit is not the same thing as a feature – and benefits are what the customer is ultimately interested in. For example:

- Feature: "This face cream contains vitamins C and E"
- Benefit: "Containing vitamins C and E, this face cream will protect your skin and prevent pollution damage – keeping you looking younger for longer."
- In this example the feature is vitamin C. The benefit is the fact that it will make you look younger for longer (hopefully!)

Think about your (current and potential customers). What benefits are they seeking from your organisation?

But don't segment your customers to such an extent that you end with unworkably small groups of people that you do not have the resources to target effectively - as author of "Marketing Plans", Malcolm McDonald, puts it "Segments must be of an adequate size to provide the organisation with the desired return for its effort" and this applies as much to the voluntary sector as to every other.

Targeting

Once you have divided your potential market into segments, you need to work out which of these are worth targeting. "Worth targeting" may not simply mean in terms of profitability, but perhaps in terms of their influence, profile or need – and certainly those seeking benefits which your organisation is set up to provide.

According to the Pareto Principle, 80% of your sales (or take up of your services) tend to come from 20% of your customers. So it's worth identifying your most "profitable" or active market segment as one of your core target markets and focusing attention (and marketing activity) on them. This **doesn't** mean that you can't also provide services for the wider (and possibly less profitable) community; conversely, by establishing a sustainable income stream through your regular, core customers, you can free up other resources to target other areas of need.

Competitive positioning

The media has recently highlighted public concerns about charities and their activities, for example:

> 'There are too many charities doing the same thing'.
> 'Too much of what the public gives to charities is spent on fundraising or administration'
> 'Surely the money we give to charities should be spent directly on their users rather than on educating the public or campaigning?'

Indeed, recent research carried out by the Media Trust found that 70 per cent of the poll believed that there are too many charities doing similar work.

> How can you differentiate your organisation?
> What sets your organisation apart?
> What do you (or could you) offer that your competitors don't, or better still, couldn't?

These questions are fundamental in establishing your "competitive position" – the ethos at the core of how you communicate your organisation.

Traditional consumer marketing identifies three main strategic choices for competitive positioning:

- Price-led
- Niche
- Differentiation (or added value)

Price-led positions are typically adopted by supermarkets and newspapers – every day commodities with little to offer by way of "difference". Such a position is rarely appropriate for voluntary organisations and can indeed be extremely damaging; not only can such strategies spark "price wars" but can also lead to the perceptions of the product being damaged – after all, if something doesn't cost much, it can't be worth much, can it?!

Niche strategies are appropriate for organisations whose basic, core service, is something that no (or few) other organisations offer, giving them an immediate, natural competitive advantage. Many smaller voluntary organisations will naturally find themselves in a niche position. However, if you are in the process of starting a new organisation, or a new strand of work and think you have found a niche market, it's worth double checking why – is it a genuine gap in the market which you can fill? Or is it too small to be viable? Have other organisations tried to fill this gap and failed – and if so, why? Niche strategies are by definition very targeted and can be quite narrow – you may therefore find that you need to do less in the way of customer segmentation (see above).

Differentiation strategies look at added value and are typically adopted by service providers; for example insurance companies may seek to differentiate themselves on the basis of customer service or claim response times. A differentiation strategy will be appropriate to larger voluntary organisations and/or those with a sub-sector competitor as they focus on emphasising what you have got to offer which is different from your competitors. Differentiation strategies are also appropriate for former niche organisations which are facing competition from new entrants, or which have expanded their remit.

Exercise: Think about your organisation. Who are your competitors? What do they offer? What do you – or could you – offer that's different?

BRANDING

Your brand is your expression of your organisation and your expression of your difference.

The brand sums up your competitive positioning – a brand is defined by the Encyclopaedia Britannica as "Any visible sign or device used by a business enterprise to identify its good and distinguish them from those made or carried by others."

The point about brand management is that it works as a kind of shorthand for the core ideas and purpose, the identity of your organisation. It carries with it a whole set of associations and values for your customers – ideally conveying positive attributes and aspirations. If you remember the point raised above that many members of the public believe there are too many charities doing the same thing, then it's crucial to make your brand stand out – indeed, this is the starting point of a differentiation strategy.

In conventional commercial marketing the elements making up a brand are things like:

- Physical attributes of smell and feel
- Aesthetic qualities of design and look

- The rational or logical parts of its usefulness
- Price
- The emotion of what it is associated with, such as having a good time, being valued by someone else etc.

In the service-led and value-driven voluntary sector, the idea of a brand in embodying abstract, intangible qualities and beliefs is particularly relevant.

It's also important to think about names of organisations. As we know names conjure up a multitude of associations and images. Think about Levi's, think about The Body Shop, and think about Railtrack. Many argue that choosing the right name is vital if we want to be able to link our organisations with positive associations. Scope changed its name from the Spastics Society in 1994 in a bid to address some of the perceived negative connotations of their name. The new Scope attracted a large number of new donors (40,000) after its name change and was also in discussion with many corporate sponsors. For your own version of brand management it is worth thinking around the core work of the organisation and the images and associations it conjures up. What is the shortest message that conveys the reality, or some of the reality of the service you provide? Is there a new logo that could be developed that would help convey the desired images or associations of your organisation?

Whatever your particular cause, the issue is still the same– how to project the image that reflects the great work that you and your organisation are doing.

Developing your brand

Branding building is a specialist process – and a time-consuming one! If you are seriously thinking about developing a new brand or revamping your existing one, make sure you allow enough time for the process. If you are making a radical change, i.e. launching a new brand or changing your name, you need to allow at least 12 - 18 months; if you are "tweaking" your logo only, less time may be needed.

Make sure you get buy in from all your stakeholders – your members, supporters, funders, media and – vitally – staff and trustees. Explain why you are thinking of rebranding and get their buy in to the process as early as possible.

Do your research - find out what your stakeholders think of your current logo and positioning. Don't throw the baby out with the bathwater – remember that although you may have seen your logo on eight pieces of paper every day for the last ten years, it doesn't mean that your customers have – ask THEM what they think.

Don't start the creative work until you've worked out your strategy and competitive position – how you want to be seen and what you want your brand to convey.

Once you've got to the creative stage, brief your designer thoroughly. Remember that a design can only be as good as the brief the designer has been given. So be as specific as possible about how you want to be perceived, what image you want to project and what you want to achieve by rebranding. If possible, get external input for the design – it's very difficult to be truly creative and objective with a solely internal perspective.

If you're changing your name and are operating internationally (or likely to in the future – and bear in mind that anything that appears on the Internet is available worldwide), make sure that any names, acronyms or graphics you choose are transferable. Failure to do this could at best mean that logos are meaningless, and at worst that they are likely to cause offence or damage your organisation (Vauxhall experienced this problem with their Nova car – Nova means "doesn't go" in Spanish. The name was subsequently changed to Corsa).

Make sure your logo and name underpin your values and work in different formats (e.g. print, web, letterhead etc)

Get stakeholder buy in – but don't try and design by committee!

Once you've got some sample designs, test them on your stakeholders to get their reaction and fine tune accordingly.

Launch your new or revamped brand as part of your organisational strategy. Although as discussed above, you want to differentiate your brand and make it stand out, it is important for voluntary organisations not to be seen to be wasting money. Launch your new or revamped brand not in isolation, but as an integral part of a strategy to meet your customers' needs.

THE MARKETING MIX

The component elements of what is referred to as the "marketing mix" are:

- Product (or service)
- Price
- Place (i.e. where or how your product or service is accessed)
- Promotion

However, most of the classical "text book" marketing terms are derived from the FMCG (Fast Moving Consumer Goods) industry and the service sector has added some additional elements to the mix:

- People
- Process
- Physical evidence

We will look at each element of the marketing mix in turn.

Product (or service)

In the voluntary sector the product may refer to a service, be this given free or in exchange for money, or to a more tangible "product" such as a publication.

The product is the core of your marketing offering – at a fundamental level it is the expression of why your organisation exists. But before developing a product or service, you need to establish the market (or need) for this service and your customers' ability to access (and, if appropriate, pay for) this service.

Establishing the need and market research

Who are your customers? What do they expect from you? Make a list of all your customers. Alongside each group add what their needs, wants and expectations of your organisation are. This process will help clarify each customer relationship you have with a group or individual.

Obtaining relevant, up to date customer research is a vital part of marketing – and business. For if marketing is fundamentally about fulfilling needs (albeit profitably), then research is about finding out what those needs are. Good market research is invaluable in assessing levels of demand, market testing, benchmarking against competitors and in tracking your progress and performance. It also has an important PR role in making your customers feel valued.

Strategic listening will underpin all of your efforts in taking an organisation or service forward. Keep asking people powerful questions such as:

- Did we say what we would do?
- Did we do what we said we would do?
- How can we do it better?

Asking these questions can help immeasurably in making your organisation transparent and accountable to its stakeholders – and over time, building greater trust and confidence in your organisation. But this is only the case if we are prepared to act on the findings. Conducting research and – as can happen all too often – letting the results sit, unimplemented, in a desk drawer, is at best a waste of time and resources and at worst, damaging to your reputation: raising customer expectations and then failing to fulfill them. Make sure you manage expectations by being explicit about what changes are possible – and what are not.

Similarly, the cost of obtaining the information shouldn't be greater than it's value to you – for example, it's not worth spending £100 on a piece of research that could only ever save you £80.

RESEARCH METHODS

The two main types of market research are:

- Quantitative
- Qualitative

Quantitative research is concerned with numbers – e.g. what percentage of your customers rate your service as excellent, good, fair, poor etc. Quantitative research usually takes the form of a survey (either postal or online, or conducted in telephone or face to face interviews), which asks a series of "closed" questions. Although some open ended (comment) questions can be included in this type of survey, they are not best suited to this type of survey, as they are expensive to analyse and do not allow for further probing of the reasons behind a particular comment. They are best used to give respondents an opportunity to give a reason to elaborate on a tick box answer.

Quantitative research is ideal when you need hard data to back up an argument or when you want to ask reasonably simple questions. To ensure that the results are statistically valid and representative, two areas are key:

- Choosing a representative – and large enough – sample of respondents to avoid bias
- Ensuring that the questionnaire is well written and that individual questions are not "leading" – i.e. written in such a way that a particular response is most likely.

If you are outsourcing your research to an external agency, they will be able to provide advice on sampling and questionnaire design. If you decide to conduct the research in house, make sure that you send the questionnaire to a wide range of (relevant) respondents and test the questionnaire on colleagues and ideally, someone who is less familiar with your work, to check that it is clear and unbiased.

Qualitative research

Typically thought of in terms of focus groups, qualitative research is a term for in-depth discussion with a small group of individuals. The point about qualitative research is not that it is representative, but rather that it allows for a richness of information and gives you the freedom to explore different subjects in an organic way, opening up areas of debate that you may perhaps not have thought of.

Qualitative research is useful if you are not sure of the issues around a certain subject and want to explore the area more. You can then test the consistency and representative ness of these views in a larger scale quantitative survey.

Conversely, qualitative research can be useful as a follow up to a quantitative survey if you want to tease out particular areas of interest in more detail.

Focus groups are best led by trained, independent facilitators with the skill to draw participants' views without giving an opinion themselves. The optimum size for a focus group is no larger than 6-8 people.

Case Study – using focus groups

Building a new village hall

Focus groups were used to get the views of local people in a village that were to build a new village hall. This was an opportunity to get the views of different age groups to see what ideas and visions they would come up with. Younger children worked with an artist to create images and models of the kind of building they would like to see. Other groups for young people, parents, single people and older people tackled this on a more verbal level in order to present ideas for what the building should look like and what services it could offer the community.

The village hall committee had a lot of money available to spend on this project, and wanted to make sure that no one could say: 'But why didn't you include a quiet area for people wanting to read or relax?' Or 'Where is the community café?'

PRODUCT LIFE CYCLE

When considering your own products it is worth thinking about the concept of the product life cycle – the idea that a product (or service) has a life cycle, which goes through the following phases:

- Introduction – the launch of a service, based on research and response to a need
- Growth – the service taking off, demand for it increasing as word gets round
- Maturity – demand has stabilised – it is reliable but not growing.
- Decline – demand for the product tails off and may eventually die off altogether, perhaps because of competitor offering or new technology, or a change in what is fashionable or newsworthy.

When you begin to think through these models and concepts in relation to your own services you can see, in commercial or survival terms that it is important to keep your products or services relevant. Ideally, you want to have at least one service in the growth stage and one in the maturity stage (which is referred to in a similar model, the Boston matrix, as your "cash cow") at any one time, plus another waiting in the wings to take their place and offset future decline. It's not necessarily that a set of needs have been met once and for all, but rather that they need to be met in a new and fresh way.

Product "layers" and added value

A product - or particularly, a service – cannot be seen in isolation; it is part of a wider experience that contributes to how the customer feels about it. The different layers of the product can be seen as:

Generic product

This is the bare bones, no frills, basic product or service – the very least the service should be providing for the money. Using a business sector example of a laundry this is about the washing and ironing of your shirts and trousers.

The expected product

This is about what the customer is likely to expect as part of the service – with shirts and trousers the expectations may include: having them packaged; having them done within a reasonable time (two days); the price being competitive with other suppliers; there being no spots or stains.

The augmented product

This is where added value, in terms of extras, comes in. We are now talking about superior customer service. This could include: sewing on missing buttons without being asked to; the shirts and trousers being delivered; a much shorter turn around of the finished articles.

The potential product

This now becomes about any crazy, new ideas which simply stretch this service into the unmatchable – this could be with the shirts and trousers being collected so you don't have to go to the shop, perhaps it could be a service where you don't own the clothes!

Today's augmented is tomorrow's expected product

If you see the four levels as concentric rings then there are significant realisations. One is that if we are looking to find competitive advantage (see positioning above) these do not come from the inner rings, they come from the outer ones. The generic and expected product specifications are taken for granted now in all sorts of commercial ways. The message now is to move beyond satisfying the customer to delighting the customer.

Generic
        Expected

                                Augmented

            Potential

Select one part of what your organisation does, be this advocating on behalf of others or delivering training for staff. Analyse this activity in terms of the four levels of customer service and see what results you come up with. Yes, even if you're not running a business for profit with customers who always pay directly for your services, and can perhaps shop around for the best deal. But it may be interesting to see what you and the team come up with. Where are you setting your sights? At the product level? At the expected? What would it take to move to the augmented level?

When I first came across this exercise I was involved in delivering training for housing and homelessness-related staff across the North of England. My example looked like this:

Generic product

The basic training course as advertised in terms of its content and usefulness

Expected

Refreshments including biscuits (you would be amazed at how many complaints you get about there being the wrong kind of biscuits or tea or coffee!) The trainer is competent, the seating is reasonably comfortable, and there is a confirmation letter with clear joining instructions. The course handouts are well produced and up-to-date.

Augmented

There is a wide range of refreshments. The trainers are the best. There is a discount on attending a further course or two courses for the price of one. The handouts are so good that you can use them in your own work. Courses are linked to accredited programmes so that you build up a good bank of qualifications for yourself.

Potential

The trainers aren't only the best; they're also really funny and dynamic in style. Policy makers are invited to the training day and accessible through video conferencing or email discussions.

Remember that customer expectations will gradually rise – either as the result of your own excellent service, or a competitor's offering. Either way, you cannot afford to be complacent, but need to commit to continually improve your service.

PRICE

The amount you charge for your products and services – even if they are free – is a key element of the marketing mix.

But it's not as simple as charging enough to cover your costs, although this is of course a vital consideration! Consider too how price affects our perceptions of value – charging too little for a product can lead customers to believe that it is of poor quality. You need to be consistent too - if you charge £1 for a four page A4 report, don't give the next one away free. And don't charge £5 for it either – this will only confuse (and alienate) your customers. Of course, you will want to make your prices accessible to your target audience, and market research plays an important role in ascertaining your customers' willingness and ability to pay. You also need to consider any competition and their pricing structure – and if your service isn't the cheapest make sure that you have a persuasive argument about why it is **better** – this is the essence of the differentiation strategy outlined above.

The discipline of costing out services and elements of services is also vital in setting out to fundraise – charitable trusts in particular will want to see a full breakdown of your project costs.

PLACE

The term "place" relates both to your physical location and to how you distribute your services – your supply chain.

If your organisation invites visits from your customers, the place needs to be one that fits with the profile of your user group. You need to know your customers and their needs well. Place needs to be accessible in terms of location and transport facilities; can users access public transport or can you provide them with transport? Another aspect of place is to make sure that your premises are customer-friendly – welcoming, comfortable and informal?

For larger voluntary organisations which rely on a branch network to provide their services, or those that run charity shops, it's important that all your branches, shops and service providers reflect your core values.

If you outsource any distribution elements (e.g. mailings, book sales etc), it's important that the suppliers provide a level of service that will reflect well on your organisation and enable your objectives to be met.

PROMOTION

Promotion is the area that people traditionally think of as marketing and the one that we hear most about. It concerns the way in which we communicate with the community and the public that we serve – how we let them know what we've got to offer. Surprisingly, this area is often overlooked – voluntary organisations with limited resources often neglect to budget for sufficient resources (time and money) to promote their services effectively and this is an area that needs to be addressed through good organisational planning.

METHODS AND MEDIA

A plethora of marketing methods and media are available and there are pros and cons for each – and their effectiveness will vary depending on your organisation, your audience, and the specific service or product that you are promoting.

The amount your spend on promotion is a difficult issue for voluntary organisations to balance: how to raise your profile, convey a sense of quality and get the results you want either on a very limited budget, or conversely, without being seen to be "wasting" money on advertising rather than your core work. This is particularly true for fundraising campaigns – direct mailshots of this sort are typically produced in "handwritten" type fonts and sent in brown envelopes to give an impression of need and frugality.

Public relations

'Public relations is a deliberate, planned and sustained activity to establish mutual understanding and goodwill between an organisation and its publics.' Institute of Public Relations

It is perhaps the case that the voluntary sector is experiencing what the public sector has faced for some time – that the public is not necessarily disposed to think favourably of them. The overall message of public relations is that these views need to be managed. If you don't do this then you run the risk of being at the mercy of other people's interpretations of what you do. Public relations can include:

- Media relations
- Customer relations
- Information
- Publicity
- Public communications
- Campaigns and promotions
- Corporate marketing

The term public relations is most generally used in relation to media activity. The huge advantage of media activity is that it is free! It also appears independent – an external verification of your claims. However, the significant disadvantage is that it is not controllable – there is no guarantee that your story will appear at all and if does, it may not appear in the way that you want it to.

Remember that public relations is not just about proactively putting out news and stories that you want to appear in the media; it is also about how you react to external (sometimes negative) stories – either maximising your opportunities or limiting damage.

Case study

Housing For All

Since we last met Housing For All much has happened. The organisation has made some genuine progress – through a combination of having such a good new director and the concerted efforts of a critical mass of existing staff that want to move things on. The vehicle has been the quality working group and the implementation of a programme of organisational change through the PQASSO quality framework. A lot of work has been done on improving key elements such as staffing and staff development and supervision, and also on involving users in organisational planning and vision.

Just at the present a new initiative has been set up which aims to explore how the Internet and online communication can benefit people with mental health difficulties – when a crisis breaks. It's discovered that a small group of staff and clients has been using the Internet to place bets online. Just as the senior staff at Housing For All find this out so does the local media, and all hell starts to break loose, with the phone going constantly and journalists approaching clients and staff for interviews.

In this new world of public relations and image management how would you, as the director of Housing For All, propose to manage this media crisis? What different issues and principles would you take into account and what specifically would you do to both contain the crisis and move things on? Give this some thought before moving on to consider the recommendations of a PR consultant.

10 commandments for working with the media

The following 10 commandments are based on the ideas of Adam Woolf (Guardian 9/11/00):

1. Don't assume the media is against you. This can set up purely defensive attitudes that tend to come over very poorly for the organisation
2. Think about how the bad press will affect your relationship with key stakeholders (or audiences) and go in for the necessary damage limitation
3. Find out the facts yourself – the truth needs to be known and to be clear – otherwise people can say what they like without challenge
4. Make sure you acknowledge public concern (e.g. over how public money may have been misused) and then remind others of the good news stories you have had
5. Respond decisively – if your organisation needs to take action, then do so decisively and publicise the fact
6. Set up clear lines of communication and areas of responsibility as to who deals with whom and how. You will have to speak with the media, but you can do so assertively and by arrangement
7. If you can make time, consider in advance how you and the organisation would deal with such a crisis. When in the full glare of unwelcome publicity the stress will be huge and clear thinking will be easier if you have thought it through in advance
8. Can you get any advance warning – perhaps by thinking of any areas where the organisation is vulnerable to negative coverage?
9. Don't forget to ask for help. As I outlined in the management competencies section, when the going gets tough we all need our allies and friends.
10. Keep things simple, straightforward and don't take unnecessary risks when things are already a little out of control.

Advertising

Unlike public relations, the advantage of advertising is that it is controllable. You have full management of how and when your message appears. It can, however, be extremely expensive! Before deciding to place an advert, ask for details of the publication' circulation, how it is distributed (mailed to named individuals or sold for example), readership profile (does it match your target audience?), forthcoming features (are there any stories associated with your work that you can tie in with to add strength to your advert?) and of course the rates. It's worth getting sent a media pack and rate card, but do try and negotiate a price rather than paying rate card – there's usually some margin for discounts!

Make sure you check what the copy deadlines are – and what format artwork must be supplied in. Can you meet the deadline? If not, does the publication offer a design service to its advertisers?

Then, try and make your advert as specific and targeted as possible. Make it stand out from the page - avoid too much copy and include an attention-grabbing visual if you can.

The success of advertising is difficult to measure. You can add codes to response mechanisms to track follow up but this is not an exact science – your customer may not remember to quote the code you've given them. Moreover, if someone happens to respond to one advert, who's to say that they weren't subconsciously influenced by the fact that they'd seen the same advert twice before? Generally, advertising makes a good back up to more direct methods of promotion.

Direct marketing

The term direct marketing is used for promotions that are sent direct to a named individual – e.g. a mailshot, an email or a telemarketing survey.

Online marketing in particular is increasing in popularity, offering an effective way of reaching individual clients at a fraction of the cost of a postal mailing. Other benefits include speed - quick turnaround times that enable you to respond quickly to external events, and almost instant response times. And you can adapt your message to specific target audiences, enabling you to tailor your promotions to smaller market segments than would be possible (or cost effective) when using traditional media. Remember too that marketing online doesn't have to be about selling something – it's also an ideal way to keep in touch with your supporters.

The main benefits of direct marketing for voluntary organisations are that it is:

- (Relatively) cost effective – you know whom you're going to contact, it's less hit and miss than advertising
- Easy to measure – you can track responses to specific campaigns by including codes or special response slips
- Targeted – you can tailor your message to meet specific customer groups. And because each letter, email or phone call is a one off, you can segment your offer

down to a far greater level of detail, far more accurately, than is usually possible with advertising.

Permission marketing

"Permission marketing" is a term relating to good practice in direct marketing (particularly direct mail and email). The 1998 Data Protection Act (which came into force in October 2001) states that consumers should be given the opportunity to opt out of receiving communications that they do not want. Permission marketing effectively goes one step beyond this, by actively encouraging customers to opt *in* to receiving communications.

But before you worry about the effect that this will have on your marketing campaigns, remember that the most effective promotional campaigns are those that are carefully targeted to key market segments – i.e. the people who are most likely to be interested in your products and services. And those customers who have opted in are likely to be the warmest of all – making your campaigns far more cost effective.

THE DATABASE

High quality data is the backbone of direct marketing. Remember that the information that you get out of your database will only be as good as that which you put in. Take time when inputting data to thoroughly profile or tag your contacts in terms of their areas of interest and preferences and update this whenever possible. This will enable you to target your offers to specific customer groups. You can also buy in lists from list brokers or agencies – if you decide to go down this route make sure that you use a reputable agency and check how the list was compiled – i.e. that the contacts listed have consented for their details to be used.

But customer details change all the time. Even well managed databases are likely to contain out of date information and you need to consider how you will deal with bounce backs from your email. Database cleaning is a slow process, but vital if you are to both improve the accuracy of your list and, even more importantly, ensure that you do not continue to mail people who have asked not to be contacted. The good news is that as you clean up your list, the number of errors should greatly reduce.

Similarly, you need to allow time to deal with responses to your mailshots. Customer expectations on response times to direct mail are high – and even higher for online marketing, so make sure you are geared up to respond and set aside time and resources to do so. Remember that a mailing that generates demand that you are unable to meet (whether this be for products, services or information) is likely to do more harm than good.

The message

Regardless of which medium you choose, for your promotion to be successful you need to get the message right.

Think first of the objectives of the your promotion – what do you want someone to do as the result of seeing your promotion? Classical marketing identifies four stages of response to promotions, known as AIDA:

Awareness
Interest
Desire
Action

What action do you want your reader to take as a result of your promotion?

Target your message to the customer segments that you have identified, emphasising how your service provides the benefits (rather than just the features) that they are seeking. Remember too that you can segment down further in terms of promotional message, for example using different wording for different types of customer.

People

Your people (whether trustees, staff, volunteers or other supporters) are the public face of your organisation – the ambassadors of your brand. It is therefore vitally important that they convey the same ethos, quality of service and customer-centricity that you are trying to portray. Remember that the best product in the world can be undermined by one bad experience on the phone – and remember too that customers are more likely to vote with their feet than to make their feelings known.

Process

How do people access your service? Is there a simple process that meets their needs? Or do they have to go through a succession of telephone calls, being passed around the organisation, before they get what they want? If you're not sure how easy it is to access your service, it's worth doing a bit of "mystery shopping" – putting yourself in the shoes of your customer and finding out what processes they have to go through. Where you can, try and make your processes as accessible as possible by offering a variety of methods to suit all abilities – for example, online as well as telephone ordering.

Physical evidence

The idea behind physical evidence in marketing services is providing something tangible. For example, this could be a course booklet, handouts from a training course or a brochure about your organisation. In a sense, physical evidence is part of the augmented product that we discussed above.

EXERCISE: THE MARKETING MIX

Focusing on your own organisation, what are your thoughts about each of the seven Ps and the resulting marketing mix?

Product
Price
Place
Promotion
People
Process
Physical evidence

6.

New technology and the voluntary sector

The use of online services within the voluntary sector is growing apace, not least because once the resource is available it can save substantial amounts of time and money and achieve things which could otherwise not be contemplated.

Working with ICT

The vast majority of people now recognise that computers have a hugely important role to play, not least as an efficient, low-cost communication tool.

Leaving aside for a moment the self-evident advantages of using computers for word processing and financial data, the benefits of being online, with email and a website setting out your organisation's aims and objectives, products, services and needs, are immeasurable.

Email has many uses: instant day-to-day communication with people and organisations world-wide, networking PR and publicity, marketing, recruitment, campaigning, fundraising and research.

Even counselling can be delivered via email, though it might seem at first glance to be completely inappropriate for the task.

For example, the London borough of Kingston-upon-Thames set up a website that offers young people access to social services via email, because it had been discovered that children were already trying to access help through the internet. It had also been found that they were not comfortable with presenting themselves in person at the social services office. Hence, this project has enabled children to contact a personal adviser via the internet and receive help and advice by the same route – and they are doing so, with no discomfort. It can also help many more children, far more cost-effectively, than would have been possible via traditional means.

So for some people or groups the medium is part of the message.

Other service users might prefer to see a friendly face before asking for help, but in this instance, and significantly, the preferred method of communication was identified through the active involvement of the young people.

That's not all. Over 50,000 people have contacted the Samaritans by email in the course of a single year. It has emerged that email is especially attractive to men. A Samaritans spokesperson said: 'Email is proving a good way for men to reach out for help as they are less likely than women to turn to friends or GPs.'

Research and information management

According to recent joint research by NCVO and BT many voluntary organisations feel that the Internet is of most value to them as a research tool. Sources of useful information include government reports and statistics (reports that cost, say, £20 in a bookshop can be accessed without payment); news bulletins, such as the Guardian Society Briefings on daily email; websites for staff involved in specific areas of work, for example, Haznet for health action zones, Regennet; academic publications and more.

Take some time to explore, to follow up links and investigate where the information of relevance and value to you is. Serendipity plays its part, but you will not know what is useful until you have had a look. As far as getting up-to-date in your field is concerned, the internet can be a great boon. Closer to home, online tools can offer cost effective, user-friendly solutions to obtaining feedback from your customers.

Fundraising on the web

Many people who use the internet regularly never come across fundraising campaigns on the web. This issue is being actively explored through, for example, a charities' internet fundraising and e-commerce forum which meets every two months with about 50 fundraisers to hear pitches from web entrepreneurs.

The schemes under consideration include online shopping malls, which pay commission to charities on goods sold if they refer customers. Gareth Edwards of the Royal National Institute for the Blind (RNIB) urges people interested to be cautious, check out the financial situation of a company that is a potential partner, and find out how and by whom the scheme will be marketed. If a lot of charities are taking part the income for each will be reduced.

Your own website, too, is a shop window where you can give information about your organisation and its work which will help you to forge relationships with donors at little cost.

Case study: Elim Pentecostal church

The Reverend Paul Sinclair transformed the situation he and his church were in through his use of the internet.

The church, the Elim Pentecostal in Willesden, was owned by the local council. The church wanted to buy out its neighbour, a bookmaker, but was getting nowhere. Then the pastor, who was a keen motorcyclist, went online and began to make contacts with motorcycling groups all round the world.

The Rev. Sinclair strongly believes that a church, as a local small business, needs outside investment or a mutually beneficial partnership: 'This is where the internet comes into its own, acting as a huge matchmaking agency. There is no other tool which is so international, cross-cultural and effective.'

Since the pastor went online to fundraise, the church has received help to buy its own building, buy out the bookies next door and much more.

Networking and new communities on the web

If you launch your own website, your message can be accessed by anyone anywhere in the world. People can learn about your organisation and the valuable work it does, find out how to contact you, discuss issues, and find out how they can get involved or donate money.

In addition, the internet enables organisations to form alliances and networks with people and organisations in related fields. Projects can share information and experience and begin to explore collaborative possibilities – a manifestation of the 'joined-up thinking' promoted by New Labour, which for the voluntary sector can mean improved ways of working, sharing knowledge and thinking. Regardless of the government's deadlines for the delivery of all government services online, the benefits for other sectors that develop their own capacity are clear.

To move our own organisations forward it is clear that change will need to happen on both the technical front and the people front. Computer networks may depend on cables, modems and telephone lines, but it is the people at each end of them who are communicating with each other. Thus the voluntary and community sector can communicate within itself, with other sectors and communities, with government, with the business community and with the media.

Communicating with volunteers and staff

The internet can act as an integrating mechanism, a glue to help personnel, whether they are working in the same premises or dispersed far and wide around the world, stick together.

Communication can be instant: the same message sent to each and every one of a designated group, all of whom can respond just as instantly. For example, one major voluntary housing association provided email links for tenants, the regional office, headquarters and housing staff. The housing staff declared email their most productive IT resource – and also the one their clients use the most.

New technology can also mean new employment opportunities – many people with disabilities can take advantage of computer technology to work productively.

Recruitment

The internet can also serve as a recruitment tool. Vacancies can be advertised on the website and applications, including CVs, received via email.

Campaigning on the web

'A key question for campaigners now is how to connect individuals with decision-makers. The most credible organisational campaigns will be those where individuals can speak for their own interests.' (Mark Flanagan of Advocacy Online, quoted in *The Guardian*). Advocacy Online was a trail-blazer interactive site, launched as the first online campaign by the United Kingdom Breast Cancer Coalition.

The internet not only allows people to speak for themselves rather than be spoken for, but has the power to connect individuals directly with decision-makers. For example, subscribers to The Guardian Society Briefings are invited to discuss issues with government policy-makers over the internet.

Practical tips for websites

- Be sure to be accurate: people will visit sites out of curiosity or need, but will return if the information is reliable
- Stay up-to-date: your campaign should be current on key developments in your field – in addition to offering your own perspective on what's happening
- Keep it clear and simple: people need to be able to absorb information quickly, then they can respond and act
- Make it easy to navigate: enable visitors to the site to be able to move around without getting lost or having to do too many clicks.
- Layer the information: write clear summaries, then add more detailed links
- Maximise interactivity: encourage others to interact with your information by using discussion boards, listserves and guest books
- Promote the site: advertise in key search engines, other websites, sympathetic projects and in paper publications
- Set up links: connect to other campaign sites and *vice versa*
- Use a good statistical engine – one that will tell you how many visitors to your site there are and where they are based – and use this data to develop the site
- Don't just rely on the net for your campaign – lots of people still aren't connected. Use all the other methods you relied on before the net arrived.

(tips courtesy of Nick Buxton of Jubilee 2000)

Developing an internet strategy

To develop your internet strategy, start by asking: 'How will being online help fulfil our organisation's mission?' Then look at the different ways the new technology will feed into specific aspects of your mission and strategic plan. One way to do this is to ask those who are already using these forums and channels how it benefits their clients, organisations and staff and volunteers. Build on the experience of others, just as you do in other ways.

Most organisations will recognise immediately that being online could add value to what they do, but they may not have the financial resources to get to that stage. Fundraising tactics could include exploring opportunities within the community, taking on board the match-making advice on pages 131-2. The business community wants to help, and wants to be seen to help. Use your local umbrella agencies so that you do not try to reinvent the wheel. In this area Voluntary Action Leads (Leeds) has found very enthusiastic take-up among small voluntary organisations to which a free modem and appropriate training are offered.

The information and technology divide

The internet offers exciting possibilities in all sorts of ways, and they need not be expensive. But many are concerned that the information-rich/information-poor divide will deepen. Those with the positive experience need to be able to explain and demonstrate the benefits to others who, for whatever reason, are holding back.

7.

Financial management

Although the legal responsibility for the financial management of a voluntary organisation lies with its board of trustees (sometimes called a council of management, management committee or steering committee) – who in unincorporated organisations are *personally* liable – all managers are accountable for the finances relating to the activities within their areas of responsibility. This chapter looks at the financial framework of organisations, acknowledging the role of the trustees in this context, and the budgeting processes and controls that support that framework.

What follows is not intended for finance directors or management accountants, but should serve to clarify the fundamentals of what needs to be done and why. Hence, the key objectives in this chapter are:

- to show that financial management is part of the overall thinking and planning cycle, and that it applies to trustees as much as employees
- to consider the Big Picture, in the form of a business plan
- to identify the key elements of practical financial planning
- to develop a feel for financial monitoring and reporting
- for trustees, to appreciate that financial management is an essential element of good governance.

Strategic planning that ignores the financial realities has no useful purpose or value. Effective financial management starts with good financial planning, an integral part of the thinking process that trustees and managers need to undertake on a regular basis (see Chapter 2). Time invested in financial planning will have a positive impact on an organisation's fundraising capacity, as it will on the ability to manage and respond to changes outside its control.

The model for strategic planning on page 53 can be built upon as follows:

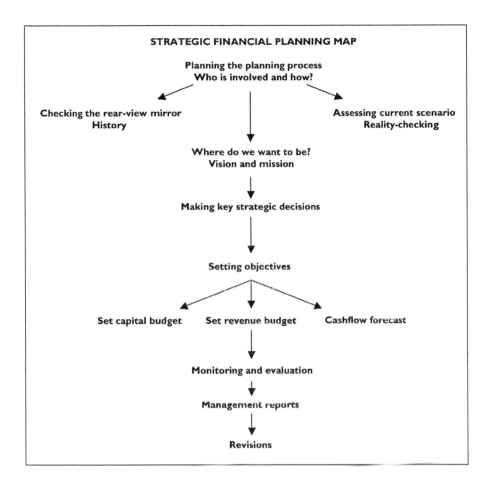

STRATEGIC FINANCIAL PLANNING MAP

Planning the planning process
Who is involved and how?

Checking the rear-view mirror
History

Assessing current scenario
Reality-checking

Where do we want to be?
Vision and mission

Making key strategic decisions

Setting objectives

Set capital budget   Set revenue budget   Cashflow forecast

Monitoring and evaluation

Management reports

Revisions

The business plan conveys the Big Picture, into which all the budgeting and forecasting carried out within the organisation feed. Business plans, covering either the whole of the organisation or one component part of it, are a key management tool, although many organisations may not produce one until required to as part of a substantial funding bid. Whatever its purpose, the business plan is basically a way to represent the strategic and financial planning clearly and concisely; indeed the financial plan – a budget – is essentially a numerical version of the strategic plan, the figures behind the words.

Not only does a business plan work to inform and convince funders, it also works to help trustees, staff, volunteers and clients to act towards the same goals. It should be a unifying and motivating force for internal stakeholders, as well as a flagship for external stakeholders, or potential stakeholders. A business plan can also be drawn up for a project within the organisation as a whole. Whichever it is, a business plan can demonstrate that the organisation is on course financially and that its core funding is enough to see it through the time period covered by the plan.

COMPONENTS OF A BUSINESS PLAN

Executive summary
A condensed version of the whole document, listing the key points in just one or two pages.

Introduction and mission of the organisation
Focusing on the organisation's mission, why the business plan is important for the organisation at this particular time, and the period covered by the plan.

Organisational background and history
The legal status of the organisation, address of its registered office, brief account of how it began and any key partners who have been influential in its development. It may be helpful to include essential information about how the services have changed and developed over time.

Current state of the organisation
The business plan is intended to inspire confidence, but should also include an honest assessment of the organisation's weaknesses and threats as well as its strengths and opportunities (reflecting the thinking carried out after a SWOT analysis or similar exercise).

The organisation and its environment
Describing how the organisation sits within, and fits within, today's ever-changing society. Is government policy influencing the work of the organisation? If so, how? Are the needs and wishes of the client groups served by the organisation changing in form or shape, and what does this mean in terms of the planning and decision-making process? The focus of this section, therefore, is on the opportunities and threats presented by forces beyond the control of the charity.

Strategic aims and objectives
Reflecting the outcome of the strategic planning process, this section specifies the aims and objectives for the work of the organisation: partly the *what*, and partly the *how*. If the organisation aims to make a difference – say, to improve the quality of life for carers – this section will explain through what specific activities this will be achieved.

Implications arising from the aims and objectives
The resulting implications could be legal, or structural, or to do with staffing numbers or fundraising and so on. If the aims and objectives have shifted through the thinking process, new decisions will have resulted. These could mean, for example, offering a new service to fill a gap, which would have funding implications.

Financial implications
This, the key financial element of the business plan, includes information on how the plan will be funded, the income and expenditure projections for the first year in detail and estimates for further years. It will include any key thinking and assumptions behind financial decisions and projections, and will refer to the organisation's marketing plan (see Chapter 5).

Action plan
A timetable for action on a step-by-step basis.

Monitoring and evaluation
Describing how the finances of the organisation will be monitored and accounted for, and also on how the work of the organisation will be evaluated, i.e. how it will gauge whether its work is having the desired impact – and hence, its approach to quality management.

KEY ELEMENTS OF FINANCIAL PLANNING

This section will cover:

- capital and revenue budgets
- analysing costs
- contribution analysis
- break-even analysis
- overhead apportionment
- cost centres
- forecasting income
- cashflow forecasts.

Capital and revenue budgets

Capital expenditure refers to larger, one-off costs for, say, property or pieces of equipment, e.g. buildings, motor vehicles or photocopiers. (Conversely, the revenue budget covers ongoing costs of running an organisation, e.g. salaries, rent, heat, light etc). Therefore, the capital budget means thinking ahead for three to five years about what will need to be purchased, when, how much it will cost and where the funds might come from. Items bought from the capital budget may have implications for the revenue budget: for example, photocopiers need to be maintained, and the cost of this will be funded from the revenue budget.

Capital budget

Expenditure

Expenditure	2002–3	2003–4	2004–5	2005–6	2006–7	Total
Premises	56,000	75,000	25,000	–	–	156,000
Office equipment	2,000	18,000	–	7,000	–	27,000
Furniture	7,000		4,000	6,000	–	17,000
Vehicles	–	10,000	–	11,000	–	21,000
Totals	**65,000**	**103,000**	**29,000**	**24,000**	**–**	**221,000**

Income

Income	2002–3	2003–4	2004–5	2005–6	2006–7	
Grants	95,000	75,000	6,000	11,000	2,000	189,000
Donations	5,000	6,000	6,500	7,000	7,500	32,000
Totals	**100,000**	**81,000**	**12,500**	**18,000**	**9,500**	**221,000**

The revenue budget is the working budget for the organisation, showing running costs and project-related costs. It is constructed from the detailed plans for all operational areas (fundraising, staffing etc.), bringing them together with the aim of matching the income to the expenditure. As well as a detailed revenue budget for the year ahead the organisation needs outline budgets for three to five years ahead.

The budget will reflect the predictions you make about *the amount of income earned less the costs incurred*. It is prepared to show the surplus or deficit which will arise if the financial plan is carried through.

Sample revenue budget with overhead allocation					
INCOME	**Project 1**	**Project 2**	**Project 3**	**Central**	**TOTAL**
Contracts	5,000	–	50,000	–	55,000
Grants	20,000	–	–	–	20,000
Fees	–	45,000	105,000	–	150,000
Total income	**25,000**	**45,000**	**155,000**	**–**	**225,000**
EXPENDITURE					
Director's salary	–	–	–	20,000	20,000
Project staff	14,359	28,717	77,436	–	120,512
Admin staff	–	–	–	18,000	18,000
Direct project costs	–	–	40,000	–	40,000
Publicity	–	1,000	–	1,000	2,000
Recruitment	–	–	1,000	1,000	2,000
Office rent	–	–	–	10,000	10,000
Telephone	–	–	–	3,500	3,500
Stationery	–	–	–	3,500	3,500
Audit and accountancy	–	–	–	2,500	2,500
Legal and professional	–	–	–	500	500
	14,359	29,717	118,436	60,000	222,512
Central admin allocated	7,375	14,750	36,875	(60,000)	222,512
Total expenditure	**21,734**	**44,467**	**155,311**	**–**	**222,512**
Surplus income over expenditure	**3,266**	**533**	**(311)**	**–**	**2,488**

Budgets, forecasts and financial reports can be produced using spreadsheet software, which will of course do all the adding and subtracting for you as long as you enter the right formulae, and can easily be updated. Be sure to back up all the data on a floppy disk (or by whatever means your organisation takes backups) so that it is not lost in the event of a system breakdown.

Cost analysis

Putting together a meaningful budget involves working out what the costs will be over the next year and beyond. A common approach is to take this year's budget and add a fixed percentage for inflation, cost of living or similar to each category, and for years beyond the one immediately ahead this broad-brush method may be the only option. But for the first financial year (sometimes, but not always, the same as the calendar year), where more is known about the organisation's plans, more thought is needed and greater accuracy can be achieved.

For example, rather than just forecasting that staff salaries will rise by a certain percentage, you could take into account the fact that a post will remain vacant for several months, which will reduce staff costs (eventually, however, recruitment costs will be incurred, and these should also be borne in mind).

The starting point for a budget is to identify the key areas of expenditure for the organisation or project. For a project running training courses for staff in voluntary organisations these might be:

Trainers' fees
Trainers' expenses
Venue costs
Publicity
Course materials
Salaries
Telephone
Photocopying
Staff expenses
Stationery

Costs are considered to be either *fixed* or *variable*. Fixed costs include the overheads and do not alter in relation to the level of activity. Variable costs change in proportion to the level of activity undertaken. For example, the training project's publicity costs will vary according to the programme of training events; the creation of artwork for its stationery represents a fixed cost, but the amount of stationery printed will vary, depending on how much is needed and when. *Mixed* costs have a fixed element but are also affected by the level of activity.

Costs can also be broken down into *direct* and *indirect* costs. This involves assessing the cost in relation to the structure of the organisation and in which part of the organisation the cost arises. *Direct costs* relate specifically to a particular project or department. *Indirect costs* are those incurred by the organisation as a whole. For example, costs for central administration are indirect as they cover all of the staff groupings and projects across the organisation. Hence, the question of whether a cost is direct or indirect is a matter of where the cost arises.

Exercise

Either make a list of the main cost areas for your organisation or take the cost areas as outlined in your budget.

Analyse your cost headings to assess whether they are variable or fixed, direct or indirect, or a combination.

Ask yourself the following:

- Is the cost incurred whatever the organisation does? For example, rent and insurance are fixed costs
- Does the cost vary depending on the level of activity? On the training project example, some of the training is delivered by salaried staff and some by associate trainers, and the proportion will vary, so this would be a variable cost
- Does the cost arise only in relation to a specific project? The training project hires venues specifically for its events, therefore the cost incurred is direct
- Does the cost vary to some extent but have a core cost which must be met? For the training project telephone calls are heavy at certain times of year, but the rental is the same whatever the number of calls – hence, these costs are mixed.

Contribution analysis

Identifying the fixed costs is the starting point for creating a cost structure for the organisation as a whole. The *contribution* or 'profit' in private sector terms that is needed from income-generating projects must match the total of the fixed costs of the organisation in order for the organisation as a whole to *break even*. Individual projects also need to cover their direct costs.

Capacity – the Regional Voluntary Sector Training and Development Group

This organisation operates a training programme, a mentoring scheme and a consultancy project for organisation development, all based in one building together with the group manager and administrator.

For contribution analysis the figures can be shown as follows:

Project costs	Training	Mentoring	Consultancy	Total
Staff salaries and NIC	12,000	9,500	13,600	35,100
Associate staff	8,000	–	–	8,000
Materials	4,500	600	1,600	6,700
Additional telephone	800	300	190	1,290
Additional printing	970	200	740	1,910
Additional travel	760	250	330	1,340
Additional expenses	450	150	175	775
Venue costs	3,300	750	–	4,050
Total direct costs	**30,780**	**11,750**	**16,635**	**59,165**

Centre fixed costs				
Group manager's salary and NIC				26,000
Administrator's salary and NIC				17,000
Premises				8,200
Contribution needed from projects				51,200
TOTAL INCOME NEEDED				**110,365**

Capacity needs a total income of £110,365, of which £51,200 are fixed costs and the remaining £59,165 relate to the projects and their direct costs. Each project has to have enough income both to cover its own direct costs and to make a contribution to the fixed costs of the organisation. The implication for fundraising is that the funds must cover both the direct costs of a project and also the contribution to the fixed costs of the organisation.

As the above chart demonstrates, contribution analysis will help you make vital decisions, such as, for example, whether you should start a new project or close down an existing one.

If, for example, one of the Capacity projects were to be closed down none of the fixed costs of the organisation as a whole would be lower; the saving would be made only on the direct costs of the project. Similarly, if Capacity wishes to start up a new project, this would have no effect on the organisation's fixed costs but the new venture would need to cover a proportion of them (make a 'contribution') in addition to its direct costs, to be viable.

There will be a limit to the number of projects that can be run from the same premises or by the core staff, and once these resources are exhausted the possibility of increasing the organisation's fixed costs by moving to larger premises, or of taking on more core staff, will need very careful consideration.

Break-even analysis

This is an extension of the process of identifying the contribution from a project or activity. For any organisation as a whole to break even the contribution from all of the activities must be equal to the fixed costs. This applies also to smaller-scale activities, so it is wise to identify the fixed costs and break-even point of activities such as fundraising events which have the potential to lose, rather than earn, money.

Example

A project group working with disadvantaged young people on a large estate plans to hold a disco in a local authority hall with a capacity of 300. The entrance fee will be £3.00 and soft drinks will be on sale at 20 pence. The door will be manned by volunteers and the drinks will be organised and sold by volunteers.

Hence, the fixed costs are:

Hire of hall	£100
Pay for caretaker	£30
Publicity leaflets	£75
Soft drinks	£30
Total fixed costs	£235

As the tickets are priced at £3.00 the organisers need to sell 68 tickets to break even. Every ticket sold above that number will yield profit. As the organisers are expecting a turnout of at least 175, they hope to make a good return on their investment. If a lot of soft drinks are sold, as is likely, the profit will be higher.

If the event does not break even, the fixed costs will be lost. So what the group needs to work out is what number of tickets need to be sold in order for the event to break even, and make this a target. Otherwise, it might have to bear the loss.

Overhead apportionment

In order to divide up the overheads over the various teams or projects within the organisation, the full cost of the various activities needs to be worked out so that the cost allocation can be carried out on a reasonable and fair basis.

To do this you first need to clarify the different types of costs for the organisation and get a picture of the cost structure as a whole. The apportionment will reflect management time, premises and central costs and administrative services. It is likely to be an estimate and be based on a measure such as:

- amount of space used
- staff costs

- staff numbers
- number of users
- income.

You might apportion the cost of the premises on the basis of the space used per team or project. The telephone costs might be apportioned on the basis of numbers of staff using the phones.

However, apportioning costs can become a matter of dispute or resentment among teams competing for scarce resources. To avoid this, the process needs to be clearly explained to all those involved. The budgets which show apportionments are used for mapping the full costs of any activity and this is useful for identifying which activities make a surplus and which need subsidising. All core overheads have to be funded, usually by being apportioned to projects and included in fundraising applications. The more costs can be directly attributed to projects the less need will there be to apportion other costs.

Apportionment and funding applications

The budgeting procedures you carry out are principally for your own benefit and as such are separate from any funding application. Both draw on the same information and thinking, but remain separate entities. How will you manage apportionments when fundraising, given that some funders will not entertain apportionments and will refuse to cover any overhead costs?

The best way to prepare a submission to a funder who is unsympathetic to the inclusion of apportioned overheads in bids is to cost in every extra cost due to that activity – all the extra phone calls, every item that will be directly used by that project from each and every staff member to the last sheet of paper and rubber band – not forgetting computer sundries. Maybe the project will not be able to contribute to the fixed costs of the organisation but it should not be a drain on resources either. If a funder questions any amount which relates to apportioning costs it is important to be able to explain them – to provide an outline of the organisation and how it works and of the process of apportioning costs.

If your potential funder has a policy which dictates a fixed percentage of administration costs, find out what it is the funder will fund in terms of administration costs and how this percentage is to be calculated. If the percentage relates to the *direct* costs of a project you need to identify as many direct costs as possible and to prepare a more detailed budget. It may be possible to enter costs which would normally go in as overhead apportionment. For example, time spent by the manager in managing the project may be allowed.

Cost centres

Overhead apportionment is done in order to spread the costs over different cost centres in a meaningful way. The cost centres could be teams, departments or projects, separate units of accommodation, geographical areas, services provided and so on. Bear in mind the revised Statement of Recommended Practice (SORP) for charities when organising cost centres. SORP obliges you to analyse charitable expenditure according to activity on the actual statement, and for to analyse other expenditure according to management, administration, fundraising and publicity costs.

Sample cost centre budget for Capacity					
Direct costs	**Training**	**Mentoring**	**Consultancy**	**Central**	**Total**
Salaries and NIC	12,000	9,500	13,600	43,000	78,100
Associate staff	8,000	–	–	–	8,000
Materials	4,500	600	1,600	700	7,400
Telephone	800	300	190	450	1,740
Printing	970	200	740	1,000	2,910
Travel	760	250	330	600	1,940
Additional expenses	450	150	175	500	1,275
Venue	3,300	750	–	–	4,050
Premises	–	–	–	9,000	9,000
Total direct costs	**30,780**	**11,750**	**16,635**	**55,250**	**114,415**
Central costs apportioned					
Premises	4,500	2,000	2,500	(9,000)	
Other overheads	24,000	9,350	13,000	(46,250)	
Total costs	**60,280**	**23,100**	**31,135**	**0**	**114,515**

Central costs are apportioned in two parts. The costs for premises are apportioned on the basis of the space occupied by each project and the remaining overheads on the basis of the staff costs for each project.

Forecasting income and cashflow

Income forecasts have to be based on reasonable assumptions. Some income will be *definite and confirmed*, for example, where a funding has been signed and sealed or a contract is running over several years.

Other income will be *probable* – for example, if funders have signalled that funds will arrive. If this includes covenanted income it is important to realise that the amount received will be less a certain percentage, which you can estimate if you have tracked this in the past. Probable income will also cover income from other fundraising methods such as applications to trusts or events such as the disco example mentioned above.

Possible income could be amounts which could be raised through new methods of fundraising not tried before or the provision of extra funds from existing funders.

The judgements made concerning future income will form the basis of the fundraising plan, which will need to project reasonable figures for income and also to cost out the costs of raising this income.

The cashflow forecast

A revenue budget focuses on the forecast income and expenditure, matching costs to the related source of funding, and shows the year-end outcome as either a surplus or a deficit. In real life, however, the flowing in of income and the flowing out of expenditure do not always match, so the cash position will vary.

This needs managing. The cashflow forecast is useful in this respect in that it is based on the information from the revenue and capital budgets and it will also forecast when actual receipts of income and outgoings will happen. The cashflow is concerned with the actual cash flowing in and out, not with which budget heading it comes under. *It needs to be regularly updated if it is to have any meaning.*

Sample cashflow forecast

	Apr	May	June	July	Aug	Sept	Oct	Nov	Dec	Jan	Feb	Mar	Total
Receipts													
Contracts													
Grants													
Consultancy													
Loan													
Total receipts	A												
Payments													
Salaries													
Inland Revenue													
Office costs													
Projects													
Loans													
Capital purchases													
Total payments	B												
Net cashflow for month	A−B=C												
Balance brought forward	D	E											
Balance carried forward	C+D=E												

Interpreting a cashflow forecast

The bottom line of the forecast shows the forecast balance at the bank at the end of each month. If it is negative the account will be overdrawn. A positive figure indicates the cash available. Ideally, you should try to time the spending of money with the receipt of income. If there are months when you might go overdrawn, try to analyse the payments and receipts due to see which (payments) can be delayed and which (income) can be brought forward.

Checklist for cashflow forecasting

- What is the pattern for income over the year?
- Is income in advance or in arrears?
- Have you made allowances for staff changes?
- Are capital payments scheduled for when the income is expected?
- Are your forecasts for income reasonable and realistic?
- If you are not registered for VAT do the figures include VAT?
- If you are registered for VAT have you prepared a VAT calculation?

CORE ELEMENTS OF FINANCIAL MONITORING AND REPORTING

This section looks at:

- budgetary comparison and flexing
- variance analysis
- monitoring cashflow
- financial management in a crisis
- presentation of information.

Financial reports are a core management tool. Different reports are needed by staff and trustees at various levels of the organisation.

Budgetary comparison and flexing

Comparing the figures in the financial plan/revenue budget and the actual amounts of income and expenditure recorded is a key monitoring procedure. It is essential to compare like with like: the same period, the same budgeting category, for example. Hence, the headings need to be the same in both accounting records and budgets – if they are not, no valid comparison can be made.

Budgets often need to be 'flexed', however, to take into account the fact that income and expenditure do not happen evenly throughout the year. To divide an annual budget figure by 12 and expect that to reflect the month-by-month reality would be naïve.

For example, if an organisation expands and takes on new staff these costs will appear at a specific point in the year. If this were to happen in the last quarter of the year, dividing the cost by 12 and spreading them across the year would be misleading. Instead, the staff costs need to be calculated for the first nine months on the basis of the existing staff and for the last three months with the inclusion of the extra staff. Thus real comparisons can be made between the budget and actual expenditure. For organisations working in situations where income and expenditure have a seasonal pattern it will be helpful to prepare budgets on a quarterly or monthly basis.

Variance analysis

A variance occurs when there are significant differences between the budget figures and actual income or expenditure. These have to be explored, by comparing information in the underlying financial plan to actual performance. Making and keeping notes that explain estimates for the budget is very valuable, especially in organisations with high staff turnover, part-time working and job-sharing. Variances are likely to be caused by:

- a change in numbers
- a change in price
- a change in timing.

Understanding the reason for the variance is essential. If there is a drop in numbers of people booking on the Capacity's training courses does this mean that the targets were unrealistic? Or has another competitor organisation has started up in the same field? Were the courses not sufficiently marketed? Will income targets need to be adjusted?

Example variance analysis at Capacity's Training Project

The Training Project is planned to be self-funding through income from staff on courses. The budget estimated income at £35,000 and the actual income is calculated at £31,850 – a negative variance of £3,150. What are the variables that explain this variance?

Course fees

Public/statutory rate: £120 per day
Voluntary organisation: £85 per day

Actual bookings

	Budgeted numbers	Budgeted income	Actual numbers	Actual income	Variance
Public/statutory	125	15,000	83	10,000	(5,000)
Public/statutory	235	20,000	257	21,850	1,850

Hence, the bad news is that the estimated number of staff from the public and statutory sector (paying more than the voluntary sector) is less than the estimate and if this is the start of a trend new decisions need to be made. In previous years the numbers of bookings from this sector had held steady, but now there is a significant drop.

The good news is that the number of bookings from the voluntary sector is up by almost 10 per cent and it may be that in the longer term the Training Project 'repositions' itself as a resource only for the voluntary sector.

Another example of a variance might involve staff costs. If the budget is for six members of staff but one leaves midway through the year and this post is not filled for five months, there will be a saving on staff costs: this would explain that particular variance.

Clearly it helps to have a deep understanding of what makes your organisation tick and also of the factors affecting it. For a project such as Capacity's Training Project the number of bookings is key, and historically the number of bookings from the public and statutory sectors has been influential. In projects running housing and supported accommodation, if properties or beds are empty this will be a significant factor and organisations will need to analyse over time the average number of empty beds or properties they are likely to have. Once this figure is arrived at, as a percentage, targets can be set in order to reduce this and thus increase the inflow of income.

Monitoring cashflow

The monitoring of cashflow may be crucial for projects heading for or in crisis. For this task an end-of-year balance sheet is needed. This shows that the accounts do balance given correct reconciliation of key balances, e.g. the bank balances. Balance sheets are structured under two headings, as follows:

Current assets (what we own or are owed)	*Current liabilities* (what we owe others)
● stock	● bank overdrafts
● debtors	● loans from others
● loans to others	● trade creditors
● short-term investments	● accrued expenses
● bank accounts	● tax and National Insurance
● prepaid expenses	● VAT.
● petty cash.	

The above items constitute the working capital of the organisation. Working capital is assessed by calculating the likely amounts under each of the headings.

From the balance sheet it is possible to progress to a cashflow forecast, which aims to predict the inflow and outflow of cash. The cashflow forecast will show the surplus or deficit amounts at the end of each month. It is important to make these forecasts as accurate as possible for several months in advance as this will enable you to make informed financial decisions, such as whether to delay payments, borrow money, put more effort into fundraising, and so on.

Financial management in a crisis

If you make your cashflow forecast a living and breathing management tool it will alert you to upcoming problems. When you revise it, you must date the revision so you do not store up confusion for the future, when you – or someone else – will be wondering what was included and what not, or which was the most recent update. The forecast will help you decide, in a potential crisis, who should be paid at once and who can be paid later, or whether to delay new expenditure on equipment or staff. A classic mistake is for the organisation to carry on spending in line with the budget without taking account of the implications for the cashflow. Another pitfall to watch out for is taking too large a risk when money is tight: for example, investing a large amount in a particular fundraising venture may be considered to be too risky and a decision to cancel or delay it may be necessary.

Pointers for managing cashflow under pressure include:

- asking suppliers for favourable terms (more time to pay)
- making some payments by instalment
- prioritising the larger payments due
- reviewing pricing policy (can you increase your prices?)
- making sure debts are paid promptly
- delaying additional expenditure e.g. on recruitment or equipment.

Any organisation facing financial crisis must analyse the reasons for it and devise a new plan which will lead it out of the danger zone. If the organisation is a limited company the directors are bound by company law to stop trading when debts can no longer be paid. Remember that trustees are *personally* liable to pay the debts of a charity if it becomes insolvent.

Presentation of information

How key information is presented is a major factor in the making of responsible decisions. The only reason for producing financial information, after all, is to encourage the making of good decisions. It also has the potential to alert people to problems and keep all those involved, including the trustees, in touch with developments. Also, the sharing of information broadens the responsibility for the accounts.

The core needs are income and expenditure statements (usually monthly); information that compares the cumulative position compared to the year's budget (usually quarterly); and details of the current cash position. Out-of-date figures are useless, and it is essential that each committee meeting should have figures up to the end of the previous month. The report must be reliable and based on monthly reconciliations to ensure the completeness and accuracy of the accounting records.

Financial information can often benefit from the inclusion of a few illustrations, such as pie charts, bar charts or line charts. These help to break up the text and make key information easier to grasp. If you are to follow up on this, you need to explore useful software packages and to invest the time in mastering these.

FINANCIAL CONTROLS

Various practical steps can be taken to create and keep good financial controls over money and assets. This section will cover:

- the need for internal controls and what they are
- how internal controls relate to the law
- how to manage external risks.

Internal controls

All organisations run the risk of mismanagement or fraud. The fewer the controls or the more lax the controls, the higher the potential risk. Characteristics of organisations which experience such problems include: an absence of formal and written policies and procedures, too much authority resting with staff who are inexperienced, trustees having insufficient understanding of their roles and responsibilities, a lack of training, managers not reporting properly to trustees, which leaves the trustees operating in the dark, the presence of ongoing conflicts between employees or between employees and trustees, and situations where senior staff have too much power and control and abuse it. Implementing good controls not only protects the assets and capital of the charity, but helps to protect staff, trustees and volunteers.

As was said early in this chapter, the monitoring of financial plans is central to good internal control. Trustees must approve the budgets before their implementation, then monitor financial performance against these budgets. To this end they must receive regular, relevant financial reports which contain explanations of any significant variances.

Compiling a financial management procedures manual

A key tool for proper financial management is a manual, a living and breathing manual with up-to-date guidelines and procedures and sample forms outlining the ways money and assets must be managed. This will be useful for the induction of staff and volunteers, for trustees and also for auditors.

Contents of a financial management manual

- Guidance on how to use the manual
- Map of organisation structure – roles and responsibilities for finance
- Financial planning and budget cycle – timetables and explanations
- Reports – what kind of financial reports there are and whom for

- Bank accounts – cheque signatories, purpose of accounts
- Income – procedures for opening post, banking money, handling cash, invoicing
- Expenditure – authorisation limits for approving expenditure, system for approving and paying invoices
- Petty cash – what this is for and to what amounts, authorisation procedures, reimbursing system and records
- Payroll – payments to staff, changes in salary rates, documenting new staff appointments
- Staff expenses – methods of reimbursing, limits of expenses and for what payments, authorisation of payments.

In addition to an up-to-date manual a sound internal control system also requires the following:

● Physical controls
Certain things should be locked away – e.g. laptop computers, perhaps some other items of electrical equipment, petty cash, cheque books. Adequate insurance cover is also essential.

● Bookkeeping
Bank reconciliations need to be reviewed on a regular basis. Invoice systems with sequential numbering of invoices need to be maintained so that their completeness can be verified.

● Authorisation and approval
Financial transactions need to be approved by people who are authorised to do this. Further, limits to authorisation have to be determined so that staff can authorise up to a certain amount themselves but must refer larger amounts to the next stage of authority. Of course, approvals should be documented with a signature or a minute from a meeting.

● Segregation of duties
The system for financial procedures should aim to prevent both mistakes and fraud. It should be be organised so that different members of staff and trustees check on each other. If there is no segregation of duties too much responsibility and power could reside with one person, but if duties are segregated different people will place orders, approve and pay for services, items of equipment, and so on.

● Supervision and training
It is vital to identify the learning needs of staff and to provide ways to address this, whether through courses run by local Councils for Voluntary Service or by internal training methods. On top of this, all staff and volunteers need active supervision and support (see Chapter 3).

Basic practical internal controls

● Cheque payments

Usually, two signatures are required on cheques, which works if the second signatory actually looks properly at what he or she is signing – but this is not always the case. It may be worth considering having one person who can sign cheques up to a certain value without the need for a second person. It is also good practice to scrutinise cheques in batches at regular intervals so that this activity can be taken seriously. The Banks Automated Clearing System (BACS), under which details of those who regularly receive payments are set up, is time- and cost-efficient and increasingly used.

● Fixed assets

The key tool for safeguarding physical assets is the *fixed asset register* or *inventory*. This lists all major items of equipment with information regarding date of purchase, cost, where it is in the building, and its condition. The document is useful only if kept up-to-date – an active responsibility to be assigned to a specific person.

● Staff costs

For most voluntary organisations, as for most operations in the public and private sectors, staff costs represent the greatest proportion of outgoings. So that money is not wasted by employing someone who is not capable of doing the job advertised, a viable system of recruitment and selection is need. Thought must be put into the job description, the person specification and the selection procedures to make sure that the person is measured fairly and thoroughly against the criteria set in advance. Once someone has been appointed he/she needs to go through an induction programme and then to be properly supervised and supported. Working without supervision works only when all is well; supervision can prevent many problems arising, or at least stop them becoming serious.

Checks are needed to ensure that staff are paid for actual hours worked, and timesheets and overtime claims should be carefully monitored.

● Expenses

Expense forms must be authorised by someone else, whatever the claimant's level of seniority within the organisation. Receipts should be attached where necessary and explanations for each amount supplied. Usually expenses are claimed monthly. Certain types of expense, especially if significant, may need to be authorised by the line manager in advance.

● Opening post

Some organisations regularly receive money through the post. Where this happens, a set procedure for opening mail is needed. Unopened post should be kept in a secure place; two people should be present when it is opened and a list made of any cash and cheques received. For extra security, the staff responsible for this duty should be rotated. Any monies received should be banked the same day if at all possible.

How internal risks relate to the law

Employment law has proliferated over the last few years, some of it EU-driven, and can be a minefield for those who do not take the time and trouble to familiarise themselves with it. From minimum wage legislation to human rights issues (including discrimination) and rules on maternity leave, there is much to get to grips with. Failure to do so could result in an employment tribunal and compensation payments.

For similar reasons, safeguards should be in place to ensure compliance with Health and Safety Regulations.

Employers have to deduct income tax and National Insurance for their employees under the PAYE legislation. Organisations must register for VAT once the income threshold is reached.

Funds that are specifically given for certain purposes must not be spent on anything else, and so checks must be in place to ensure this happens. Legal penalties apply if charities do not comply with the rules that govern them.

The use of *internal audit* will help to ensure that proper procedures and checks are installed. The audit can bring about suggestions for improvement as well as highlighting shortcomings in the organisation's effectiveness. Internal audit should examine all the operations of the organisation, especially thoroughly in relation to higher-risk areas. It is important to remember that only companies and Industrial and Provident Societies limit directors' or members' liability. With limited liability directors and trustees are protected if the organisation becomes insolvent, unless they have been negligent or allowed assets to be used for purposes outside the charitable objectives of the organisation.

If a charity has significant contractual obligations, e.g. employing staff or leasing/ buying premises, it is worth thinking about setting up a company for this purpose as early as possible. Incorporation means that the charity is a separate legal entity and only the assets of the organisation, rather than those of individual trustees or directors, are at risk if the organisation becomes insolvent.

External risks

Sometimes situations arise over which the organisation has no direct control. A SWOT analysis (see Chapter 2) can be used to identify the 'threats' to the organisation, which might come about in a variety of ways – legislative changes, political changes, loss of funding, legal action etc.

Ways to guard against external threats and risk include:

- always working towards the enlargement of the organisation's income base. If you are dependent on one source of income this makes you very vulnerable to any changes imposed by the funder. Many charities have suffered the consequences, including those that relied heavily on local authority funding

- creating financial reserves or a contingency fund to help your organisation manage in times of crisis. Organisations with high fixed costs are particularly vulnerable and need larger contingency funds to meet the threat of reduced income
- avoiding long-term commitments to expenditure (which could include, for example, a long-term leasehold agreement) where no long-term commitment to funding exists
- insurance – not just against theft, fire and flooding but employer's liability (compulsory if the organisation employs staff and recommended if it has volunteers).

The business framework

Your financial plans and controls should, of course, link up with your organisation's mission, strategic planning and resources, as discussed earlier in this guide, and your business plan will underpin the whole.

Further reading and resources

Introduction

Compact – Getting It Right Together. Home Office, London, 1998

What Are Management Standards? an introduction, Management Charter Initiative

Best Value: a guide for voluntary organisations, NCVO, London, 1999

Best Value Performance Plan: a summary, The Media Unit, Leeds City Council, 2000

"To Mutual Advantage: getting the best out of best value", NCVO, London, 2001

"Mutual Obligation: NCVO's guide to contracts with public bodies", NCVO, London, 1998

NCVO website: www.ncvo-vol.org.uk/main/gateway/regions

Research Quarterly, NCVO, London, July 2000

Skills Matter, Voluntary Sector National Training Organisation, 2000 (to receive information from VSNTO email vsnto@ncvo-vol.org.uk)

The UK Voluntary Sector Almanac 2000, NCVO, London, 2002

Chapter 1: Personal management competences

Covey, Stephen, *Seven Habits of Highly Effective People,* Simon and Schuster, London, 1989/1992

Skinner, Steve, *Assertion and How to Train Ourselves,* CETU, West Yorkshire, 1993

Ken and Kate Back, *Assertiveness at Work: a practical guide to handling awkward situations,* McGraw–Hill, London, 1991

Roger Fisher and William Ury, *Getting to Yes,* Arrow Books, London, 1987

Gareth Morgan, *Images of Organisation,* Sage, London, 1986/1999

C. Mabey and P. Iles (eds), *Managing Learning,* Routledge, London, 1994

Rosemary Stewart, *Managing Today and Tomorrow,* Macmillan, London, 1991

Henry Mintzberg, *Mintzberg on Management: inside our strange world of organisations,* The Free Press, 1989

Hank Williams, *The Essence of Managing Groups and Teams*, Prentice–Hall, Hemel Hempstead, 1996

The Relationships Foundation, 3 Hooper Street, Cambridge CB1 2NZ

Chapter 2: Managing activities

The Good Trustee Guide, NCVO, London, 1999

Sandy Adirondack, *Just About Managing: effective management for voluntary organisations and community groups*, London Voluntary Service Council, London, 1992

Nigel Gann, *Managing Change in Voluntary Organisations – a guide to practice*, Open University Press, Buckingham, 1996

Mike Hudson, *Managing without Profit: the art of managing third-sector organisations*, Penguin, London, 2000

Rosabeth Kanter, 'Managing the Human Side of Change' in *Management Review*, USA, April 1985

Alan Lawrie, *The Complete Guide to Business and Strategic Planning – for voluntary organisations*, Directory of Social Change, London, 1994

Kurt Lewin, *Field Theory in Social Science,* London, Harper and Row, London 1951

Suzanne Lynn-Cook and Harry Zutshi, *Action Guide for Developing and Using Statements of Purpose in Residential Care*, Local Government Management Board, Luton, 1993

Gareth Morgan, *Images of Organisation*, Sage, London, 1986/1999

Laurie Mullins, *Management and Organisational Behaviour*, Pitman, 1995

Managing Activities and Resources, Open University Business School, Milton Keynes, 1995

Gerry Smale, *Mapping Change and Innovation*, HMSO, London, 1996

The SCCD Charter, 2001, http://homepages.nildram.co.uk/~sccd/sccdchar.htm

Sandy Adirondack, *The Good Governance Action Plan*, NCVO, London, 2002

Tim Pickles and Penny Sharland, *The Toolkit for Managers*, Pavilion, Brighton, 1999

Karen Legge, Chris Clegg, Sue Walsh (eds) 'The Learning Company' in *The Experience of Managing*, Macmillan, London, 1999

For up-to-date legal information see Sandy Adirondack's website: http://sandy-a.dircon.co.uk

Chapter 3: Managing people

Andrew Hind, *The Governance and Management of Charities*, Voluntary Sector Press, London, 1995

Tony Morrison, *Staff Supervision in Social Care*, Pavilion, Brighton, 1996

Steve McCurley and Rick Lynch, *Essential Volunteer Management*, Directory of Social Change, London, 1994

C. Molander and J. Winterton, *Managing Human Resources*, Routledge, London, 1996

Mike Hudson, *Managing without Profit: the art of managing third-sector organisations*, Penguin, London, 2000

Gill Taylor and Christine Thornton, *Managing People*, Directory of Social Change, London, 1995

Philip Hope and Tim Pickles, *Performance Appraisal: a handbook for managers in public and voluntary organisations*, Russell House, Lyme Regis, 1995

Lynette Hughes and Paul Pengelly, *Staff Supervision in a Turbulent Environment: managing process and task in front-line services*, Jessica Kingsley Publishers, London, 1997

P. Hawkins and R. Shohet, *Supervision in the Helping Professions*, Open University Press, Buckingham, 1989

Chapter 4: Managing quality

Self-assessment Workbook: measuring success at www.ncvo-vol.org.uk/main/about/does/qs_systems.htm#saw

Approaching Quality: a guide to the choices you could make, Quality Standards Task Group, NCVO, London, 2000

British Quality Foundation: helpline 023 9265 8828 (Excellence Model)

Excellence in View: a guide to the Excellence Model, NCVO, London, 2000 or via NCVO website

Investors in People, via Investors in People UK, 7-10 Chandos Street, London W1G 9DQ; www.investorsinpeople.co.uk

Farley, Tony PQASSO (first edition), Charities Evaluation Services, 1997, www.pqasso.org.uk PQASSO (second edition), Charities Evaluations Services, 4 Coldbath Square, London EC1R 5HL

Practical Quality Assurance System for Small Organisations, CES, 1997/1999

Best Value: a guide for voluntary organisations, NCVO, London, 1999 and http://www.local-regions.detr.gov.uk/bestvalue/inspection/gloss/htm

Social Audit, see http//www.socialenterprise.co.uk/social.htm

Anna Coote and Naomi Pfeffer, *Is Quality Good For You?*, Institute for Public Policy Research, London, 1996

Quality First: Quality Assurance Management for Community Organisations, Birmingham Voluntary Services Council, 138 Digbeth, Birmingham B5 6DR (free to community groups in Birmingham)

Links to People Excellence (explaining links between the Excellence Model and Investors in People), via British Quality Foundation or Investors in People

Chapter 5: Marketing and public relations

An organisation carrying out research in the community field, Business in the Community, 44 Baker Street, London WIM 1DH or via http://www.bitc.org.uk

Guardian Society Briefings: Linda Steele, 'Social Work on the Web', 19 December 2000; Patrick McCurry, 'Fundraising on the Net', 9 November 2000

Moi Ali, 'Marketing', Chapter 8 of *Voluntary Matters: management and good practice in the voluntary sector*, ed. B. Palmer and E. Hoe, Media Trust and Directory of Social Change, London, 1997

Dick Fedorcio, *Public Relations for Local Government*, Longman/IPR, London, 1999

Malcolm McDonald 'Marketing Plans, how to improve them, how to use them', Butterworth Heinemann.

Chapter 6: New technology and the voluntary sector

'The Voluntary Sector and the Internet' via http://www.ncvo-vol.org.uk/main/help/volnet.html

Nick Buxton, 'Top Ten Tips for Campaigning on the Net', *The Guardian*, 16 November 2000

'Weblife – on a Net Mission from God', *The Guardian*, 28 September 2000 and via http://www/fasterpastor.com

Chapter 7: Financial management

Kate Sayer, *Financial Management – for charities and voluntary organisations*, Directory of Social Change, London, 1998

Haroon Bashir, *The Good Financial Management Guide*, NCVO, London, 1999

Paul Palmer, *The Good Financial Management Training Manual*, NCVO, London, 2001

Alan Lawrie, *The Complete Guide To Business and Strategic Planning – for voluntary organisations*, Directory of Social Change, London, 1994

Sandy Adirondack, *Just About Managing: effective management for voluntary organisations and community groups*, London Voluntary Service Council, London, 1992

Paul Palmer and Elizabeth Hoe (eds), *Voluntary Matters: management and good practice in the voluntary sector*, The Media Trust and The Directory of Social Change, London, 1997

National Council for Voluntary Organisations

Details of all current NCVO publications can be found in our catalogue – call the voluntary sector Helpdesk on 0800 2798 798 or email helpdesk@ncvo-vol.org.uk to order your copy.

Index